101 Ways I Have Tried to Make Money
Or Things I Learned After It Was Too Late

Diana Dunaway

Published by BookLocker.com, Inc., Bradenton, Florida, U.S.A.

Printed on acid-free paper.

BookLocker.com, Inc.
2016

First Edition

Dedication

This memoir is dedicated to my husband, Gary,
and to my sister, Karen.

DISCLAIMER

This book details the author's personal experiences with and opinions about finance and ways to make money. The author is not a licensed financial consultant.

The author and publisher are providing this book and its contents on an "as is" basis and make no representations or warranties of any kind with respect to this book or its contents. The author and publisher disclaim all such representations and warranties, including for example warranties of merchantability and financial advice for a particular purpose. In addition, the author and publisher do not represent or warrant that the information accessible via this book is accurate, complete or current.

The statements made about products and services have not been evaluated by the U.S. government. Please consult with your own Certified Public Accountant or financial services professional regarding the suggestions and recommendations made in this book.

Except as specifically stated in this book, neither the author or publisher, nor any authors, contributors, or other representatives will be liable for damages arising out of or in connection with the use of this book. This is a comprehensive limitation of liability that applies to all damages of any kind, including (without limitation) compensatory; direct, indirect or consequential damages; loss of data, income or profit; loss of or damage to property and claims of third parties.

You understand that this book is not intended as a substitute for consultation with a licensed financial professional. Before you begin any financial program, or change your lifestyle in any way, you will consult a licensed financial professional to ensure that you are doing what's best for your financial condition.

Acknowledgments

I am grateful for the input and encouragement I received from Janice Gary, award winning writer and author of *Short Leash* and teacher of a memoir writing class at the Annapolis Senior Center, Annapolis, Maryland, and from my fellow classmates. Without the help and encouragement I received from them, this book would not exist. I also want to express my sincere appreciation to my friend, Eileen Mattingly for a wonderful job of content editing and to Robin Gilliam, author of *Gift of Desperation,* for her publishing advice.

A Few Words about This Memoir

I began writing this memoir in 1990 when, at age 48, I moved from Austin Texas to Washington DC for an entry level training job with the Federal Government. I rode a bus to work with "20 something" kids starting their first career. Packed in the bus cheek to jowl, the line, "What's a nice lady like you doing in a place like this?" came to mind. As I mused about the path that brought me to this place and time I decided to make a list of all the ways I had tried to make money.

My full-time day jobs were very trendy. I was a social worker in the 60s, a bureaucrat in the 70s, entrepreneur in the 80s and a technocrat in the 90s.The rest of the items ran the gamut from selling rocks to the neighbors at age five, to working at Yellowstone Park, to running carnival games, reading palms, selling dog tags and flying hot air balloons. Looking at the list I had to laugh, both at the absurdity of the items and at the memories invoked. Just for fun, I decided to write the stories behind the jobs on the list.

Periodically between 1990 and 2010 I pulled out the list and added to the stories. The memories of the facts and foibles, failures and successes never failed to make me laugh. In 2010 I joined a memoir writing class and began sharing the memories of *The 101 Ways I Have Tried to Make Money* with my classmates. They laughed too.

I planned to make the stories sequential in time but ran into a problem. Since my focus was not on getting a job but on ways to make money to buy the good things in life many activities overlapped.

Except for survival jobs, most of the things I've done have been to pay for a major purchase such as school, a house or a trip; to support a hobby; or for fun. My real goal has not been the money but what the money can buy.

I hope you enjoy reading this memoir as much as I enjoyed writing it.

Table of Contents

01 ROCKS

I was five years old when I became aware of the importance of money in our time. It was a dark and stormy night.... Actually, it was not. It was a dark and stormy day. We lived in Casper, Wyoming, where winter temperatures reach 20° below zero. One particularly bad day my mother sent me to the store to buy two carrots. She explained she wanted two carrots and that I was to return with the change. When I stepped off the porch, I disappeared into a four-foot snowdrift. Extricating myself from the drift, I was sure I would die before I reached the store, but I did not.

I told the grocery clerk that I needed two carrots. He handed me two bunches of carrots. I said, "My Mom wants only two carrots, not two bunches." He said, "You must be mistaken, carrots are sold by bunches." He gave me a bunch of carrots and took all the money.

The trip home seemed even colder than the trip to the store. I could hardly wait to get into my nice warm house. When I arrived, I gave Mom the bunch of carrots, told her what the man said, and explained that he took the money. She burst into tears and said, "That was all the money I had until payday. I needed the change to pay the milkman." She told me I had to go back to return the bunch of carrots and insist that the man sell me only two carrots. Back into the dark and stormy day I trudged, vowing that somehow I would earn money so I would never have to make a trip like this again.

The question that remained unanswered was, "How do you make money?" I knew that my daddy made money, but I had no idea how he did it. I would ask him and then I would know what to do to make money.

That evening, when my father came home, I asked him what he did to make money. He explained that he was a geologist who worked for an oil company. He talked for quite a while but all I really understood was that he sold something that had something to do with rocks. As near as I could figure out, he sold rocks. That was great! I loved rocks and had my own collection of them. After all, they are very beautiful. It just had not occurred to me that people would pay money for rocks. I could do that! Rocks are free! All I had to do was find them, then sell them to the neighbors! My future income was assured!

The next day I set out with my rock collection to make the rounds of the neighborhood. Business was spectacular. At each house I knocked on the door, then politely asked the person who answered, "Would you like to buy some 'rokths'." (I couldn't pronounce "s" yet.) The response was overwhelming! Almost everyone bought one rock—some more! Soon all my rocks were gone and my purse jingled with change. I could hardly contain my excitement as I imagined the wonderful thing I could buy.

My enthusiasm and my first career was short-lived. When I arrived home, mother was waiting for me. She knew what I had been doing—some of the neighbors told her. She said that I was not to sell rocks anymore, "Nobody wants to buy your rocks." I said, "That's not true. Everyone wanted to buy my rocks." I showed her my empty sack and my full purse. She said people bought the rocks, not because they wanted them, but because I was so cute they could not tell me no. I said, "I thought people bought them because rocks are so pretty." She agreed that they are pretty but explained that only some rocks are considered valuable. She said, "People can pick up their own pretty rocks."

In my rock collection, I had jade and turquoise stones I had not tried to sell. Those rocks were so pretty I wanted to keep them. Mom explained that they are called precious stones because everyone wants to keep them. They are the stones people will buy. I was not to sell pretty rocks ever again unless they were precious stones. What an awful realization! It seemed that the only kind of rocks I could sell are the ones I want to keep!

This ended my first career, that of a rock salesman. (NOTE: This incident pre-dated the "Pet Rock" craze and the plethora of New Age rock shops. Who knows, if Mom had not ended my budding career, I might have plenty of rocks today!)

My first job had not been a total waste. I did have the money from the rocks I sold before my mother stopped me. I learned it was possible to make money by selling something and it was possible to find something for free to sell. The next step was to find a new product.

2 FLOWERS

Finding a new product to sell turned out to be more difficult than I thought. Everything I thought of to sell cost money to buy. If you have to have money to make money, what good is that? Surely there must be another way! There must be! How can anyone ever make money if you have to have money before you can make money? It did not make sense to me.

I kept looking for the magic product that people would buy that did not cost anything and I found it— FLOWERS! Like rocks, flowers are beautiful. Like rocks, they are free. People like flowers. I always picked flowers for my mother and she loved them. They grew everywhere, but people did pay money for them. I had seen a florist shop. Flowers would be perfect! I went out and started picking flowers.

This career did not even get off the ground. The neighbor, who owned the flowers I was picking, called my mother to complain. Mom retrieved me from the lady's yard and tried to explain to me why I could not pick the flowers. She said they belonged to the neighbor. That seemed ridiculous to me. How could anybody own what GOD made?

Then mother tried to explain private property, how people owned land and what was on the land. The whole concept seemed somewhat bizarre to me, but I did understand that I could not pick and sell the flowers in the neighborhood. Not only that, but if people owned the land, I could not go around picking up everything I found. That would be stealing and I did not want to do that! That meant I could not "find" a free product to sell and would have to find another way to earn money.

3 GRASS

One summer day a couple of boys came to the door and asked Mom if they could mow our lawn. Because the grass really did need mowing, I was quite surprised when Mom told them no. It seemed it was very nice of the boys to offer. I asked her why, she said no. She explained that if she let the boys mow the yard, she would have to pay them. PAY! What was this?! You could be paid for doing something for someone? "Yes," Mom said, "its normal for people to pay other people to do things for them.

At last - a way to earn money! I would mow lawns. We had a very old, rusty, hand-push lawnmower in the garage. I could use that. The problem was, I was not big enough to reach the handle, and not strong enough to push the thing on concrete, much less grass. This called for a change of plans. I asked my sister to work with me. She was three years older and taller. After much discussion, I finally convinced her to try it. Off we went, down the street with the push mower and a rake.

Unfortunately, a neighbor did hire us to mow their very large yard. I have never worked so hard in all my life! It was hot, sticky, yucky work. No wonder people paid other people to do it! My sister was mad that I had talked her into this mess and I was not happy either. What I learned from this was another reason why I wanted money: so I could pay someone else to do my yard work! Oh well, scratch another bright idea!

The yard work ordeal taught me that I could make money by selling a service. The catch here was the type and amount of work done in exchange for the money! Besides, at age 5, there were not many things people would hire me to do and my sister was no longer speaking to me. I had better figure out some other way.

4 - # 7 SOME OTHER WAYS

Housework, Dishes, Ironing, Kool-Aid Stand

My fifth year, I spent a great deal of time trying to figure out "some other way" to make money. Some ideas did not work out and my parents rejected others. For example, when I learned that people were paid for housework, I asked Mom if she would pay me for the work I did. She said, "You are paid. You get free room and board plus an allowance." I asked her if other people would pay me. She laughed and said, "You are too little." She said that I would have to wait until I got bigger and learned more. I did not think I was too little and vowed to learn everything about housework.

The next day, as a surprise, I decided to wash dishes. The first problem was how to reach the sink. The stool was high enough for me to reach the sink but not the faucets. We had a double sink, so I climbed into one half and filled the other with soapy water and dirty dishes. I sat down on the counter and reached in for a plate. It was very heavy and slippery. I could not rinse it because half the sink was filled with water and my feet were in the other half. I could not put it down because I was sitting were the rinsed dishes were supposed to go. While I was trying to figure out what to do with the plate, I dropped it and it broke. That solved one problem but created some other problems. I decided Mom was right. I was too small, at least for dishes. Maybe ironing.

I plugged in my Little Miss Iron and got out my favorite apron. When the iron heated up, I spread the apron on the ironing board and put the iron on the apron. Much to my horror, an iron-shaped hole appeared in the apron. The apron MELTED! It was plastic. I learned that before you could be paid for ironing, you had to learn what fabrics could be ironed. I did not want to ruin anyone else's stuff, so I abandoned that idea.

When summer came, the next great idea was a Kool-Aid stand. To entice customers, I gave away free samples. This didn't work because after they drank a glass they didn't want to buy one. Then I drank the rest.

A promising idea that Mom would not let me do was to sell a drink I made. I loved to put a Coke in the freezer until it was partially frozen. Then I would take a fork and mash the frozen part with the unfrozen until I had a smooth mix. Mom said nobody would buy these. Ha! Someone should tell that to 7-11. They came out with my idea about 20 years later.

Then there was real estate. My folks were buying our house, so I knew people did that. One day we were driving in the mountains. I saw a sign advertising land for $2.00 per acre. I saw a subdivision where none existed. "Buy that," I said. Mom said, "Don't be silly, no one would want that land." Years later, I drove by the tract. The subdivision was there, just as I saw it.

8 SCHOOL FAIRS

When I started kindergarten, I was introduced to the school fair. This was an activity sponsored by the parents and teachers to raise money for the school. Each class had to come up with an idea that would make money for the school. Since I was always looking for ways to make money, I had the perfect idea. My Mom made the neatest stocking dolls. When my friends saw mine, they all wanted one. I told the teacher that my mother would make stocking doll for sale at the fair.

The teacher thought it was a great idea. Unfortunately, my mother did not think it was such a great idea. She explained that it was important to keep promises so she made the dolls because I promised that she would. However, as she toiled day and night to get the dolls made, she made it clear, in no uncertain terms, that I was never, ever to volunteer someone else's time, money and effort without talking to them first. The dolls sold out immediately.

Many of my friends did not get a doll and asked me if mother would sell them one. Since I had received a recent lesson in volunteering other people's time, I told them I would ask. I had visions of mother becoming rich as a doll maker. She did not. Until her death 50 years later, she reminded me of the incident.

9 SAVINGS BONDS

When I was 6, my school held a savings bond drive. We were each issued a book with places for stamps. Stamps, which cost 10 cents each, were sold one day a week. The book had a place for 125 stamps ($12.50 worth). The teacher explained that when the book was full it could be exchange for a twenty five dollar US Savings bond. Twenty-five dollars! Why, that was a fortune! After some difficult computation, I realized that was double what the bond cost. Boy, what a good deal! You did not have to work; you could get your money to work for you! I started saving my money to buy stamps.

I got only 25 cents a week allowance so it took me over a year to get the book filled. However, I figured it was worth it to give up some picture shows and ice cream cones. With $25.00 I could buy a lot of ice cream, chocolate milk and olives. I was so excited when the big day came and I got my bond. However, there turned out to be a catch. I could not cash in the bond immediately. I had to keep it for ten years before it would be worth $25.00. Ten years might as well be eternity for a seven-year-old. This was another plan that did not quite work out as expected.

When the bond finally matured, I was a destitute college student. Although I could certainly put the cash to good use, I decided to spend the money on something I really wanted. I went to the bookstore and pretended that the $25.00 was all the money I had left in the world. I bought *The Pro*phet by Kahlil Gibran, *Think and Grow Rich* by Napoleon Hill and some short stories by Mark Twain: something for the soul, something for the mind and something just for fun. With the change, I bought an ice cream cone.

10 GIRL SCOUT COOKIES

Selling Girl Scout cookies was my next sortie into making money. It turned out very well, at least for the Girl Scouts. When our troop leader told us we could keep part of the money we made selling the cookies, I thought she meant I would be able to keep part of what I made. This was great! Just what I had been looking for, a product I could sell!

I was the best sales girl in the club. In fact, I bought some of the cookies myself. They were more expensive than store-bought cookies, but I figured that since I could keep some of the money, it would cost about the same in the end. Imagine my surprise when I learned that I did not get to keep any of the money. The "we" she meant was the troop.

Oh well, I did get a ribbon for my effort and I learned some lessons: People will pay more for a product if it is for a good cause; If your goal is to make money, understand what's in it for you before you commit.

11 CAMP SYLVANIA

In 1951, when I was 9, my neighborhood in Casper, Wyoming was split between Protestants and Catholics. Families on my side of the street were Protestants and the ones on the other side were Catholic. That is, all except one family where the man was Catholic but the wife and kids were Protestants. Whenever we kids got into an argument, the Catholic kids always said, "You are going to HELL because you're not Catholic." This would result in a scream-out with the Catholic kids on their side of the street and the Protestant kids on ours. The kids from the split family stood in my yard and yelled at the kids across the street to stay out of their yard. The argument usually ended when the Catholic father came home and ordered his kids to cross the street and come home or when my sister started crying, "I don't want to go to HELL," and ran into the house. I would run after her to assure her that she was not going to "HELL" because she was a Protestant. If any of us were going to "HELL" it would be the Catholic kids for telling a lie.

The kids from the mixed family were sent away all summer to a camp called Camp Sylvania. They would return with tales of horseback riding and crafts. I was green with envy and wanted to go too. My parents said they could not afford to send me to camp but this did not make sense. After all, based on what the kids said, my dad made more money than their dad. I bothered my mother so much she finally told me why the kids from the mixed family went to camp. She said, "Catholics are not allowed to divorce or to marry someone who is divorced." They sent the kids away in the summer because the Catholic man's parents came to visit and he did not want them to know that his wife had been previously married. That put a whole new slant on my desire to go to camp. I still wanted Camp Sylvania but I did not want my parents to send me away. At age nine I decided to start my own Camp Sylvania.

We had a large back yard with an old chicken coop we had turned into a playhouse and a fishpond we had turned into a sandbox. There was a screened-in back porch for rainy days and a clothesline to hang sheets for plays. I decided it was the perfect location for the camp. Campers were no problem. All I had to do was sell the idea to the other neighborhood kids. Since I had both a younger and older sister, I decided the camp would be open to all age groups. As I did not have any money, supplies were a problem but it did not occur to me to charge for camp. I decided to worry about that later. Camp Sylvania opened for business that afternoon.

The venture became a huge success. All the kids wanted to come and all the parents loved it. Much to my amazement, the parents were also willing to buy supplies for us and to provide refreshments. What a deal! All summer long we worked on arts and crafts projects and practiced for a play to be given for our parents at the end of the summer. We made favors (match boxes covered with construction paper and decorated with macaroni) and a program. We got dress-up clothes from all the mothers and built tents for naps by hanging sheets on the clothesline. We had everything except live horses. We did have horseback riding class every day but the "horses" were only broom sticks. I ran the show and maintained discipline by threatening expulsion from Camp Sylvania for kids that acted up. The few kids I had to expel begged to be readmitted and behaved themselves when I graciously relented. It was wonderful and we all had a good time.

I was constantly amazed by the parent's generosity. At the time, I did not understand why they were so willing to give me more than I asked for, but I did understand that I had figured out a way to get the things I wanted without money. Things happen because people want them to. Therefore, create a situation where other people WANT to do what you want to do. I also learned that it was not money I wanted but the things that money can buy.

Both lessons shaped my financial future long after I figured out why the parents were so willing to support Camp Sylvania. Years later, it dawned on me that what I offered at Camp Sylvania was free day care. Of course, all the parents loved it! They knew exactly where the kids were and what we were doing. I kept the kids entertained and away from home all day. If I had charged admission or charged the parents for baby-sitting I would have made enough money to pay for everything and had some left over. Oh well, we did have fun and I learned a new way to get what I wanted.

12 MAKE A DOLLAR GROW

When I was twelve, my family moved to Billings, Montana, and I joined Rainbow, the girls' club for the Masonic Order. Its purpose was to teach us social graces and the skills we would need to become productive wives in a capitalistic society. Most of the clubs I belonged to solicited donations or sold stuff to raise money, but not Rainbow. We were each given a dollar bill and told to make it grow. Make it grow! What in the world did they mean? Was I supposed to plant it? No, I was supposed to figure out some way to use the dollar to make more dollars. I did not know what to do.

Fortunately, one of the other girls came to my rescue. Her mother suggested that several of us pool our money to rent a storefront and have a rummage sale. It was a great idea. We all scurried around getting donated stuff from friends and neighbors.

On the night before the sale, my friends and I carted the junk to the store and spent several hours sorting, labeling, and arranging things. There was an unusual appliance that looked like the horn from an old model T and another that looked like a three-headed flower vase with flexible hoses. None of us knew what either item was but, because they were so different, we decided to use them as the centerpiece for our window display.

Imagine our chagrin when the mother of one of the girls identified the "horn" as a breast pump. We hastily rearranged the window to feature the "flower vase." This, as it turned out, was an opium pipe. I learned more that day than how to make a dollar grow.

On the day of the sale, business was great. Unfortunately, no one brought any sacks for purchases. We did have old newspapers and straight pins that we brought to attach price tags. Therefore, we improvised. We wrapped purchases in newspaper and used straight pins to hold the package together. I was not very good at this, but I was good at selling.

Towards the end of the day, some reservation Indians came into the store. There was a tribe near Billings that lived in the "old way," refusing to wear the white man's clothes or talk his language. Except for me, the girls and their mothers refused to wait on the Indians. I did not understand this. After all, they were customers. Their money was as good as anyone else's. While everyone watched, I stepped forward to wait on the Indians.

When the first woman was ready, I made a very bad job of wrapping her purchases in the newspaper. After watching me for a while, she shoved me out of the way and grabbed the package. With a rapid thump, thump, thump she had the package neatly wrapped and tucked without using any pins. I was impressed! How did she do this wonderful thing? I asked her to show me. She shook her head, no, looked at me in disgust, and left the store.

After the Indians left the store, the girls and their mothers gathered around me. I had become their hero. Several people commented on the way "that Indian" shoved me out of the way and said she had no right to do that. I thought she did. I could not wrap the package and she could. I really respected her ability to do that and wished I could learn how.

My group made the most total money with our dollars but another girl made the most money for an individual. She used her dollar to buy a roll of copper wire. With the wire, she made a beautiful piece of jewelry. She sold that, and then used that money to buy more wire to make more jewelry. Her jewelry was so beautiful she had stores asking to sell her stuff and was well into making a fortune at age 12. I spent my allowance buying jewelry from her.

13 CHILD CARE

Nanny, Babysitter

Although I had taken care of my little sister all my life (it seemed), no one wanted to hire me to take care of their kids until I turned 13. My first real babysitting job was as a nanny on a two-week trip with a family to watch their five-year-old daughter. I was not paid any cash but I got a free trip to Seattle, Washington.

For those of you who have ever taken a two-week car trip with a five-year-old, you know how "free" my trip was. Talk about a nightmare! I thought MY family was dysfunctional! After spending two weeks with THAT family, I had to re-evaluate my own family. We were the Brady Bunch or the Waltons in comparison. Take my advice, if anyone ever offers to pay your trip expenses in exchange for being a nanny, demand cash by the hour. You will need it to pay for the sanitarium when you get home.

For the next four years, I averaged five nights a week as a babysitter. This is not a way to get rich, but I thought it was an excellent way to earn money while doing my homework. I learned a tremendous amount about children and learned more about the neighbors than I really wanted to know.

Because of my babysitting business, I always had money to buy what I wanted and to lend to my mother and sisters when they came up short. My favorite family was a couple who had moved to Montana from Texas. They had graduated from the University of Texas and lived for a while on Galveston Island. I thought that was so neat. I used to have daydreams about going to the University of Texas and living on an island.

I quit babysitting when I found boys, or more precisely, when they found me. I decided I preferred to spend my evenings in the company of a man-child, rather than a boy-child. In addition, I ran into problems with the fathers of the children for whom I sat. Some had roaming fingers as they drove me home late at night. My babysitting career ended one rainy night when the streets were flooded. A drunken dad was driving me home when he suddenly stopped in the middle of a flooded street and tried to kiss me. I guess he thought I would not jump out of the car because of the water. We had a mini-tussle in the front seat of the car as I told him I would tell his wife. He said, "You wouldn't do that, would you"? I said, "No, but I WILL tell my mother and she WILL tell your wife." That sobered him instantly and he took me home.

Me at Age 13

14 JUNIOR ACHIEVEMENT

In junior high, I joined a club to learn how business works. We were to design, develop, manufacture, and market a product. My group decided to sell a gadget to open jars. It was quite ingenious. I still use mine to this day. Unfortunately, it was not a product we could manufacture ourselves. It was made of metal and we had to pay too much to have it manufactured in the quantity we sold. If mail order had been available then, we probably would have made a mint. As it was, we all had to ante up money to cover the debt. The club folded.

Except for the bankruptcy, the first club experience had been positive, so I joined another group. This club's product was a chip to start fires. We made them from saw dust and candle wax, a very messy process. Manufacturing was not much fun but did avoid the expense of having someone else make the product. The chips burned easily but with a great deal of smoke, so there were not many repeat customers. Between the manufacturing hassle and the lack of sales, the second club folded for lack of interest.

What I learned in the process was that starting your own business could be risky. Your product needs to sell for more than you paid for it and it needs to be something people will actually buy more than once.

15 - # 20 BEAVER SKI LODGE

Kitchen Help, Waitress, Dishwasher, Maid, Hostess, Tour Guide

When I was 17 and in my junior year in high school, we moved to Denver Colorado and I signed up for French. In America, it is difficult to learn a foreign language because we do not hear it spoken. Most foreign language classes have about 30 kids. If all we did was talk, there would be less than two minutes per student per class to speak. As for hearing, listening to 29 other students ruin the language does nothing for one's accent.

I had grandiose plans for travel in Europe and really wanted to learn French. My next-door neighbor was in the class, so we studied together. Her father, who spoke fluent French, tried to help, but had trouble staying in the same room as our mid-Western twangs slaughtered the musical language. In self-defense, he proposed a wonderful plan. Friends of his owned a ski lodge in the Colorado Rocky Mountains. At the time, skiing was not a popular sport in America. There were few lodges and the lodges that did exist hired employees from Europe. He arranged for us to leave school for the months of November and December to work at the lodge. We would receive three dollars a day pay, plus free room, board and lift tickets. The terms of employment were that we were to speak nothing but French while we were there. What a deal! Golden opportunities to get out of school, have fun, and make money! The French part might be hard, but we figured we could cheat a little on that.

We chattered happily all the way to the lodge. The Colorado Rockies are gorgeous and the lodge was a beautiful log chalet nestled in a snow-covered valley. The owner and employees were waiting for us as we tumbled from the car. We were so excited that we ran to greet them, only to be met by stony silence. We looked at them, then back to my friend's father, who was bring the luggage from the car. He laughed and reminded us that we were to speak French. Oh yeah, that part. In a subdued mood, we turned and said, "Bon jour." The reaction was immediate. They greeted us warmly and showed us to our room, a loft up under the eaves of the lodge. For the rest of the month, all conversation with the employees was in French. This led to a few mix-ups, like the day I added sugar, instead of salt, to the soup, but as a whole, it worked out well.

Our day began at 4:00 am. We went to the kitchen to help the cook prepare breakfast by cutting, chopping, mixing, baking and cleaning. When breakfast was ready, we set the table and waited on the guests. After breakfast we cleared the tables, and washed the dishes. Then we cleaned rooms. Next we returned to the kitchen to repeat the process for lunch. From two until six, we were free to ski. At six, we returned to the lodge. One of us worked in the kitchen, while the other acted as hostess for happy hour. Guests drank hot buttered rum, spiced apple cider, and ate hors d'oeuvres. In the evening we were tour guides for the guests for sleigh rides, ice-skating or moonlight rides on the lift.

I learned to ski the hard way. The first day, I put on my skis and asked (in French), which way to the lessons. I thought I was told to go with a lady who had just rented skis. She was heading for the big lift. This seemed a very progressive start, but I went along to the top of the mountain. Fortunately, for me, the instructor was not one of the employees from my lodge. He spoke to me in English.

Obviously the worst student, I kept falling and rolling while everyone else stood up. Finally, the instructor said, "How did you get into this class? You are the worst skier I have ever seen." I told him, I thought I was doing fairly well, since I had never been on skis before. He turned white as the snow and informed me that this was an expert class and we were on an expert slope. Suddenly, the base of the mountain seemed a long way off. Although he was worried, he said, "Don't worry, we will get you down somehow." Many bruises latter, I was hugging the ground at the base of the mountain. I never learned to snow plow, but I did learn to ski, and more important, how to fall and stop.

By the end of the trip, I spent all my earnings on ski rentals, lost ten pounds and could speak French—at least, if the conversation had to do with cooking, cleaning or washing dishes.

21 DOLLY MADISON ICE CREAM PARLOR

My first real job at age 16 was working at a Dolly Madison ice cream parlor in Denver, Colorado. (To me, a real job is one with regular hours and a paycheck, rather than cash.) For a part-time job, this was a dream come true. Not only did they pay me, but I could also eat all of the ice cream I wanted and make fountain treats exactly the way I wanted, with lots of ice cream and syrup. Everything was great, until I got my first pay check. A chunk of money was missing. This was my first experience with income tax and Social Security, not a pleasant surprise.

The store manager was a little old lady who reminded me of the cafeteria manager in the Archie comics. She employed three teenagers to work the soda fountain and serve ice cream. Her theory was, if employees were allowed to eat what they wanted, they would grow tired of ice cream and not eat any at all. The other employees reached that point. I never did. The other kids were from disadvantaged homes who worked so their families could eat. I was the "rich kid" of the bunch. I kept my money and spent it on what I wanted. Since part of what I wanted was ice cream, I saved a lot of money working there.

The manager's mission was to teach us the ways of business. Although I tried her patience, I remember her, and the lessons she taught, fondly. She was a stickler for the cash drawer, insisting that "George would get dizzy" if he was not lined face up in the same direction as the other one-dollar bills. She also believed in segregation. The ones, fives, tens, and twenties were rigorously separated, as was the change. Woe be unto the employee who made George dizzy or mixed a dime with the quarters!

I was careful not to make George dizzy. In fact, to this day, I make sure all the bills in my possession are sorted face up in the same direction. However, another favorite speech of the manager's was on how many scoops of ice cream should be in the barrel. This did not make sense to me. The number of scoops in the barrel depended upon how much you scooped at one time. One of my scoops equaled three of hers, and so the seeds of my expulsion from Paradise were sown.

I made orders for customers the same way I made them for myself. Soon, I became the customers' favorite employee. They would line up, by the droves, waiting for me while the other employees stood idle. I did not understand why they got mad at me, nor did I understand why the manager's response was to lecture me about the number of scoops in the barrel. After all, the customers were happy. I was obviously doing a good job. If the other employees wanted customers, they could do what I did, and what did that have to do with the number of scoops in the barrel?

When winter rolled, around, business at the ice cream parlor dropped considerable. Most of the time, we all stood around doing nothing. When a customer did come in, I was always the first to move to the counter. When the manager talked about the slow business and the need to reduce staff, it never occurred to me that I might be the one laid off. After all, I did all the work and could easily run the place by myself. Therefore, it was a shock when she told me I was the one to go. To date, it was the only time I have been fired. Her explanation was that I was the only one who did not need the money. She also said she could save money if I left. When I asked her what she meant, she said I did not get enough scoops out of the barrel and I ate the profits. She consoled me by saying that I was a good worker, and could return in the summer.

I consoled myself by thinking about the weight I could lose. (I'd gotten a little chunky, what with the free ice cream and all.) In addition, I thought about the relevance of the number of scoops in the barrel and eating the profits. Then I remembered the Kool-Aid stand. It seems I failed to learn that lesson. If you expect to make money, you cannot give away your product or consume it all yourself. You will eat your profit.

22 INVENTORY

My senior year in high school, my family moved from Colorado to Houston, Texas. When I came home from school one day, Mom told me the local five-and-dime store needed someone to help with inventory. I did not know what inventory meant, but since I was always looking for ways to make money, I went to the store. The manager explained that inventory meant they had to count everything in the store. He said the IRS made them do it every year. I was amazed! Did the IRS have any idea how many things there are in a five-and-dime? I did not know the IRS made people do things that cost money.

Later I learned people take inventory to keep from paying IRS more money, but at the time, I blamed the IRS. What a boring, yucky job! This was a short-term job that I thought would never end. I got so tired of crawling around on my hands and knees as I counted through every nook and cranny of that store. Think of that next time you look at the bins in a five-and-dime.

At the end, the manager thanked me and told me I did a good job. He promised to have me back the next year. I thought, "Not if I can help it!" Some ways to make money are not worth the time and effort.

23 GIFT WRAP

One part-time job I enjoyed was gift-wrapping at Christmas time. A large department store near our home hired seasonal help to wrap packages. I loved it. Not only did I get to see what people were getting for Christmas, but I got to make beautiful packages. The store had huge rolls of pretty paper and yards and yards of ribbon. I learned to make bows and how to wrap a neat package. (Remember my previous experience wrapping packages?). The service was free, so customers were generally appreciative, and I made money besides. We also got a discount at the store. Such a deal! I could save money by buying. So I bought myself broke and came home with less that I made.

Have you noticed a pattern here? If I had seen the pattern then, I would be rich today. I considered money as a means to an end. With money, you could get all the neat stuff you wanted. If you want money, you have to spend less of it than you make. In other words, money gets you all the neat stuff you want, but if you buy all the neat stuff you want you don't have the money. There seems to be some sort of carousel here.

24 ELDER CARE

Remember babysitting? Elder care is a variation where, instead of taking care of a child, you take care of an elderly person. Depending upon the person, this can be very enjoyable and profitable. Many of my friends had elderly grandparents living with them. Where health is an issue, this can be extremely confining for the family. Hiring a sitter is one way the caregiver can get away for a few hours, or even a few days.

When I was a senior in high school, my first experience was when the family of one of my best friends wanted to take a vacation, but grandma wanted to stay home. They paid me to keep her company for a week. Later, when she became ill, I sat for a few hours at a time to give the family a break. This is not only a good way to make some extra money but a good thing to do as it really helps the family. As the baby boomers age, this will become a growth industry. In fact, you could probably make a business by organizing such a service.

25 PET SITTING

If you like animals, and I do, this is a service that gives benefits as well as bucks. People always need someone to take care of their pets while they are on vacation. Some people even pay to have their pets walked. My first pet-sitting job was to take care of a parrot. I had always wanted a bird, so I was thrilled when the neighbors asked me to watch Polly. As it turned out, I was even more thrilled when Polly's parents came home. Polly's favorite trick was to scatter birdseed and poop everywhere. Cleaning the cage and the house was no fun. What I learned was that I like furry pets better than feathered ones. Over the years, I have cared for cats, rats, dogs, ferrets, hamsters, and even one skunk.

26 CASHIER

I graduated from high school in 1960 and began looking for my first full time job. I found that if I told people I planned to attend college in the fall they would not hire me. It was a hard lesson to learn because I had been taught to tell the truth. You have heard that "The truth will set you free." Unfortunately, on the job front, the truth can end your opportunity for employment.

For a seventeen-year-old, full time jobs were not that easy to find. I got lots of practice filling out applications. One day I went to at least 17 companies. I know this number because when I got home I had a collection of 17 pens and pencils I had absentmindedly placed in my purse.

Finally, I was hired as a cashier for a cafeteria near my home. I was to work twelve hours a day, six days a week for 75 cents an hour with two meals a day provided; $54 per week was not great, but was minimum wage at that time. With the extra hours and the meals I thought I would do OK. Boy, did I have a few things to learn!

The cafeteria was segregated. The line employees were little old white ladies on Social Security. The kitchen employees were all African-American, many of them elderly. This was 1960, before the Civil Rights Act. White employees were allowed to eat in the air-conditioned dining room; black employees were allowed to come into the dining room to fill a single small plate with food but they were required to eat in a hot, dingy, dirty room off the kitchen. Having moved to Texas the previous year from Colorado, where there were few African Americans, this was my first experience with segregation.

My first shock came on the first day of work. The manager said employees were to use the butter plates instead of the dinner plates. He said I could eat as much as I wanted, but I could only use one plate and go through the line one time. He also said employees could select only certain foods. (In other words, you could eat as much of the stuff you did not want as you could pile on a small plate at one time.) This did not seem right to me, but since they were giving me the food, I thought. "Oh, well. I guess it's OK".

Then I got my first paycheck. Instead of the $54 I expected I got $28 and some change. They deducted money from my pay for the food! This meant I was making about 38 cents an hour. Some further calculation told me the sales price for the food allowed employees was less than the money they deducted. If they paid me, and let me buy what I wanted, I would end up with more money. After I got over my shock I suggested this to the manager. He acted very uneasy, but said he could not do that. Something was not right here. I decided to check into it.

I talked to the other employees about the limit on food and the deduction. They all agreed that it was not right and probable illegal. I called the local employment commission and, without giving names, found out that it was indeed illegal. The first thing I did was to tell the other employees. I expected them to join me in demanding our rights from the manager. Instead, the elderly explained that they could not complain because Social Security limited the amount of money they could earn. If they complained, the manager would report their jobs to Social Security and they would lose their pensions. The black employees, not on Social Security, were afraid they would lose their jobs. They all begged me not to report the cafeteria to the employment commission.

Since I still lived at home, I did not have to have the job to survive. I compromised by informing the manager that I was aware of the law. After that, I ate what I wanted, when I wanted and I used the dinner plates. I also refused to enforce the choice rule or plate rule on other employees. If they had the nerve, they could eat whatever they wanted. Most of the employees did not have the nerve. The manager was afraid to say anything to any of us because he knew he was violating the law.

The cafeteria turned out to be sweatshop. As the cashier, I was the only one allowed to sit down. Everyone else had to stand. Since we were only busy around meal times, employees would stand for hours with nothing to do. I filled my spare time by reading the Great Books of the World. Most of them, such as The Scarlet Letter and Moby Dick, were required reading in my high school English class. I had made an 'A' in the class but never read a book. I completed my papers by reading Cliff Notes and Classic Comics. Since I did not have anything better to do in the cafeteria, I decided I would read the real thing.

Another incident that shocked me had to do with segregation. It was mid-afternoon and the cafeteria was empty. I looked up from my book to see two elderly white women with a black attendant come down the line. One of the women had a walker and was having a very difficult time. They had only two trays, but from the selections, it was obvious to me that the black attendant planned to eat with the white women. I knew the cafeteria did not serve black people and I had been instructed not to check any through the line. However, there was no one else in the dining room. I could not imagine that it would make any difference. I took their money and let them pass. A few minutes later, the manager rushed to my side and informed me that there was a BLACK person in the dining room. I told him I knew, but it was obvious that the white women needed her. He demanded that I inform the black woman that she could not stay. I refused and told him that, if he wanted her out, he would have to tell her himself. He gave me a look of stark terror. I did not think he would do anything, but he did. When he told the white women, I expected them to be indignant, but they were not. One of the women said, "But what are we to do? We have already paid for the food." The manager suggested that the black girl could eat in the black employees' dining room. He said I would show her the way. They agreed.

I was horrified. As I explained earlier, the black employees' dining room was a hellhole. I could not believe people could treat other people that way! I carried her tray and apologized. She told me, "That's OK, I am used to it". USED TO IT! How could you ever get used to that sort of treatment?! That incident, plus the food deal, made me a hero to the downtrodden denizens of the establishment.

Another incident that made me a hero was the day the coffee urn exploded. The urn had a double wall. To keep the coffee warm, the space between the two walls had to be full of water. A clear glass tube registered the water level. One day, there was an ominous hissing sound as a stream of steam escaped from the urn. An explosion followed. When the coffee urn blew, I ducked below the cash register. Ceramic cups and saucers surrounded the urn. Missiles were flying everywhere.

When things quieted, I stood up to find injured old ladies, blood and glass everywhere. Everyone, including the manager, was hysterical. I did not panic. I grabbed the first uninjured lady, gave her a shake to get her attention, and then sent her to the telephone to call for assistance. This act brought the rest of the uninjured to me. I organized them to assist the people who were bleeding and began cleaning up the mess. After that, everything went smoothly. The ambulance came and took the coffee lady, the only person injured badly, and the cleanup was accomplished. As I finished sweeping the last of the broken glass, I congratulated myself on how well I handled the situation, and then I saw one last drop of blood and promptly fainted.

Fortunately, three months passed very quickly. At the end of the summer, I told the manager that I had received a scholarship for college. I said I was sorry, but I would have to quit. I think he was relieved to see me go before I organized his employees to strike. For my part, I was eternally grateful that I did not have to spend my life in such a place. The best part of this job was that I worked so many hours I did not have time to spend money. Therefore, I achieved my objective of saving money for college.

27 MARRIAGE

(Note: Previous sections are more or less sequential. This section covers most of my life)

In the sixties, a woman's route to money was to inherit it or marry it. In my case, it did not work out exactly that way. I grew up with Cinderella stories and expected to marry for love. My father told me he wanted me to go to college because he wanted me to marry a college man. He said, "I will pay for two years, and you'd better find a husband in that time." My family and I both expected me to become a housewife and mother.

My freshman year, 1960, I went to Texas Technological College in Lubbock, Texas, to earn my Mrs. Degree. If you remember, my family had moved from Colorado to Texas during my senior year in high school. I wanted to go to the University of Colorado at Boulder, but my folks could not afford the out-of-state tuition for me because my older sister was already out-of-state at the University of Wyoming. Knowing nothing of Texas terrain, I picked Texas Tech because it was as close to Colorado as I could get, and because the demographics showed four men to every woman. My, my, another life lesson in store....

For any of you familiar with West Texas, you know that it is exceedingly hot, dry and windy. To give the rest of you some idea of the place, there is a Texas song called, "Happiness is Lubbock, Texas, In the Rearview Mirror of Your Car. There is also a saying: "Fort Worth sucks and Lubbock blows." When the wind blows, the dust blows. It seeps through windows, doors and cracks and settles on everything. The Colorado Rocky Mountains it is not.

Lubbock is reputedly the site of the first EPA suit in Texas. There are stockyards to the south of town and when the wind blew from the south, the smell was awesome. As the story goes, the EPA sued. In typical Texas fashion, the suit was settled when the owners of the stock yard installed Air Wick deodorant spray dispensers (you know, like the ones they used to put in public rest rooms) on the posts around the yard. When my family moved to Texas from Colorado we spent the night in Lubbock. My younger sister's first comment on getting out of the car was "P.U., somebody here must have had a dog." Welcome to Lubbock!

I remember places by the people who live there, however, and Lubbock has some of the nicest people in the world. Unfortunately, for my purposes—remember, I was told to find a husband—I soon learned that of the four men for every woman, three of them were cowboys and the fourth was already married. In fact, my first fiancé was a West Texas cowboy who sold insurance. Fortunately, I took him home to Houston before we wed. As part of his job my father's company paid for a membership to a country club and to the Houston Petroleum Club. This was before the "urban cowboy. Although probably right at home now, at the time, the string tie and cowboy boots did not fit well at the Petroleum Club or the country club.

Shortly after the trip I gave him back his ring. It was probably for the best. He ended up selling insurance in Hobbs, New Mexico. I could have ended up a housewife married to an insurance salesman living out in the middle of nowhere.

On the other hand, I could have married rich and retired to the Houston social register. One of my high school boyfriends played polo with Prince Philip and took me to all the debutante balls. He proposed my freshman year in college too. I liked him but I didn't love him so I opted to stay in Lubbock.

In 1964 I choose to marry a man who recently finished a master's degree and had a high- paying research job at the University of Texas Medical School in Galveston Texas. Voted most popular in high school and most likely to succeed, he was successful at everything he tried. I thought he hung the moon. Three days after we married, he quit his job and enrolled in graduate school for a Ph.D. in anatomy and I joined the PHTS (putting hubby through school) club. A month later, a deputy sheriff showed up at the door to arrest him for bouncing a check to the University. I took over paying the bills and instituted an austerity program to pay off his debt and keep us out of the poor house. He turned out to be a professional student, who, I suspect, married me for MY money, or at least my ability to earn money.

My ex-husband was extremely bright, creative, and hyperactive. He had 50 million interests and hobby activities. For example, he played multiple musical instruments, had a first class electrician's license and a ham radio operator's license, collected stamps, built model rockets and planes, and raised orchids. A model train layout occupied the space that should have contained a washer and dryer and the car could not live in the garage because of the wood and metalworking equipment, not to mention the biplane under construction.

When I took over paying the bills the stringent budget did not have much room for funding hobbies. His response was to apply for (and receive) various grants, stipends, and scholarships that allowed him to continue his interests. He applied for, and received, a scholarship to pay his school expenses with a stipend of $300.00 a month for living expenses.

His first grant application was to research the function of the pineal gland. This got him the funds to setup a laboratory, complete with one of the first desktop computers, an animal lab, a darkroom for photography and $60.00 a month for a lab assistant. That may not sound like much in today's dollars, but minimum wage at the time was a dollar an hour. Guess who he hired as his lab assistant? That is, until I accidentally wiped out six months of research. Part of the project required post-mortem weighing of rats' pineal glands and ovaries. These are very, very tiny organs. From my perspective, he failed to explain how to handle fractional weights. I rounded and he exploded.

Two years later when he was completing his doctorate, we both looked for jobs. My first job offer was as Director of Hospital Admissions at John Sealy Hospital in Galveston. The pay was excellent and I was very tempted.

I had a friend who worked in hospital administration. He explained the route to success: For the first six months do nothing. Tell people you are studying the situation; For the next six-month, paint the offices and arrange for new furniture; At the end of the first year, you will receive a promotion because you had not made any enemies, you had not gotten in anyone's way, and you gave them something.

I watched him use this plan successfully. Since my husband was graduating in less than a year, I expected us to leave Galveston. I turned down the job because I did not think it would be fair to the hospital. My mistake! As it turned out, not taking the job was not fair to me. Remember that you are working for your own benefit, so consider yourself first.

My husband received numerous job offers including one to set up an anatomy department at a medical school in Thailand. I was really excited about the offer because at that time, jobs overseas were tax-free and the cost of living in Thailand was very low. They also offered a choice of routes coming and going which meant we could schedule a world tour with the job.

My second job offer was with the federal government. This was another one I turned down to my eventual regret. When my then-husband started looking for a job, I took a test that qualified me for a management intern position with the federal government. The pay was spectacular for the day. I was offered jobs, not only in this country, but all over the world. We matched on job offers in Thailand, the Netherlands, San Francisco, Atlanta, Chicago, Kansas City, Washington, DC and Puerto Rico. I wanted my husband to take the Thailand job because between us, we would be rolling in money. He was very upset because, with a master's degree and Ph.D., he was being offered the same money I could make with three and a half years of college and work experience.

He turned down all offers and decided to enroll in medical school. I pleaded with him to go to medical school in one of the cities where I had a job offer and could support us in the life style we both wanted. He refused and registered at the University of Texas Medical School in Galveston. This meant I would have to either turn down my job offers or leave him. Since my career goal at the time was to be housewife and mother, I turned down all my offers as well—in retrospect, another mistake.

My first husband and I were married eight years. By 1972 he had completed his Ph.D., his medical degree, and his internship, and was starting a residency. The previous year I asked for a divorce. He told me I should wait, that he was almost out of school and that things would be better. I waited a year. When things had not changed, I asked for a divorce again. He left the house, returned with a gun and told me he had not decided if he would kill me or kill himself. I left the next day while he was on call at the hospital.

The old saw is that men marry women to put them through school, then divorce them for a younger model. In the '70s, the trend was for women to divorce their husbands. If you could support yourself, why would you want to stay in a relationship that doesn't work? If I had stayed I would end up with a bigger house, a faster car, and more jewelry, but that was not enough. There is nothing worse than being lonely with someone. You might as well be on your own.

I was his first wife. In the ensuing years, he completed residencies in four specialties and re-married several times' I understand for a grand total of eight wives. After the first four divorces he asked me if I wanted to come back. My answer was always, "No." The last time I saw him he asked me, "Why didn't you remarry?" I said, "Why would I want to?" He said, "Was being married to me really that bad?" I said, "Yes." He said, "Why didn't you tell me?" I said, "I tried." His response was, "Well, I knew you bitched a lot." No wonder he was a serial monogamist. He obviously never learned to listen. I stayed single for 27 years.

(Note: Although marriage did not turn out to be my path to financial freedom, in 1999, at age 57, I remarried, this time to a very nice man who also worked for the federal government. The top Civil Service general pay classification is a GS 15. As I was a GS 14 and he was a GS 13, we joked that between us we became a GS 27 family. Although not rich, this certainly put us soundly in the upper middle class.)

28 SCHOOL CAFETERIA

(Jumping back from 1999 to 1960)

In 1960 my folks had paid for room, board, and tuition for my first year in college. Because I had not had time to spend it, I had the money I made working as a cashier to pay for books and spending money. Being alone for the first time in my life gave me the opportunity to spend money without interference from my parents. The first week at school, a jewelry store near campus advertised a going–out-of-business sale. (The store was still there a year later when I left.) They had wonderful stuff. By the time I bought Christmas presents for myself and all my family and friends, I no longer had money for books or anything else for the remainder of the year. Oops!

Not to worry. I reported to the college financial aid office. In the days before Pell Grants and student loans, they helped you find a job. Because of my prior cafeteria experience, I got an immediate job that paid my room and board, working in the dorm cafeteria. I received a full refund of my parents' money. The hours were great, only two hours a day at lunch and dinner. Because my parents did not think I should work they took a somewhat dim view of the arrangement but I got through the year without asking for more money and I still have the jewelry today.

The only incident at the cafeteria was a repeat of the coffee urn incident. However, this time, my star did not shine so brightly. At this cafeteria, the coffee urn was across from the serving line. It was the same type as the one before, water jacket and all. Toward closing time, we were standing around talking. I heard the same ominous hiss and saw the steam rise. I knew that if someone did not add water quickly, the urn would blow.

Like a true hero, I grabbed the largest girl standing next to me and propelled her towards the pot. She asked what I was doing but went along. When we got there, I reached around her and turned on the water, thus averting disaster. Then both she and I realized what I had done. I was mortified and she was angry. I cannot say that I blamed her. It is still one of my most embarrassing memories. It taught me something about myself I would just as soon not know.

Oh, I almost forgot to tell you about my major. Since this book is about making money and college is supposedly about preparing you for a career to make money, I guess I should at least mention something here. In the early '60s, there were not many career options for women. Women were expected to marry and stay at home with their children. The main reason women went to college was to meet and marry a man with a college education. Teaching was one career option available, though in my mother's day, women had to quit when they got married. In my day, they did not force you to quit when you married, but it was expected you would quit when you had children and return when the youngest child started school. That way you would keep the same hours as your children. Anyway, teaching was my first major.

My first experience in teaching came sooner than I expected. The college offered placement tests for some subjects. If you passed, you went to special accelerated classes. I passed the math test and ended up in a Theory of Math class. I had no trouble with the class, but for most of the people, this class was a bear. The class included 10 from my dorm, but I was the only one who was passing. The other nine girls decided it was the professor's fault and asked me if I would teach them. I tried, Lord knows, I tried! I did ever thing I could think of to explain the concepts and theories. My reward was nine pairs of eyes staring at me in dumb confusion. I started seeing those eyes in my dreams. By the end of the year, I resolved to find another major.

29 - # 32 BAR-K GUEST RANCH

Wrangler, Chef's Assistant, Bartender, Desk Clerk

I was 18 at the end of my freshman year in college when I returned home to learn that my father had arranged a summer job for me at the Bar K Guest Ranch outside Austin, Texas. This was a dude ranch owned by an oil man who was a friend of his. Before it became a greeting (as in, "Hi dude!"), the term was the name cowboys used for city slickers. A city slicker is a person who lives in a city and does not know thing one about ranch life. A dude ranch was a working ranch that took in paying guests; today, it would be called a resort. Dad said they were willing to hire me sight unseen because I had previous resort experience. (Remember the ski lodge?) He said I would love it because they had horses. I could not understand how working at a ski lodge qualified me for a job on a ranch, but I did not have any better prospects, and I certainly qualified as a "dude."

My introduction to the ranch was quite spectacular. My family drove me there and, as we pulled in front of the lodge, the door flew open. A man wearing cowboy boots and a chef's hat ran out of the lodge. Close on his heels, intent on stopping his progress, came a woman swinging a meat cleaver. A crowd of people followed her. My father recognized the owner of the ranch and called to him, but he was too intent on catching the woman with the cleaver to respond. Fortunately, they did catch her before she caught the man in the chef's hat. The ensuing scuffle and bad language that issued from the melee caused my Mom to cover my little sister's ears.

When things settled down, the owner explained that the lady with the cleaver was the wife of the man in the chef's hat, the chef for the ranch. A high school graduating class had come to the ranch for their spring retreat. The chef's wife found him in bed with the class valedictorian. Consequently, the wife attempted to murder her husband and the school canceled the vacation for the class. After hearing that explanation, Mom demanded that I return to the car. She told my father and the owner that she would not let me stay. The owner assured her that he had fired the chef and that he and his wife would soon be gone. Dad talked her into letting me stay. It turned into a very interesting and educational summer, but my mother was right—I should have gotten back into the car.

The ranch employed a strange assortment of characters. The wrangler was an elderly cowboy called Mossy, who looked, talked, and acted as if he had ridden out of a Western movie. In fact, he was the genuine article, a real "Texas Cowboy." Part of my job was to assist Mossy with the horses and the dudes. He adopted me and did his best to teach me how to ride, rope, play checkers, drink hard whiskey, and spit.

The owner hired a replacement head chef and a dessert chef who had retired from the Houston Cork Club. (The Cork Club was one of Houston's premier private clubs.) The two of them had worked together for years, constantly fighting like cats and dogs. Part of my job was to assist them. From them, I learned an extensive vocabulary of cuss words, plus how to cut, chop, cook, and bake.

I was to substitute for the bartender and desk clerk on their days off. We became good friends and I learned that they were gay. I taught them what I knew about makeup and dress. They taught me how to mix drinks and to keep books. Personally, I think I got the better end of that deal. I also served as tour guide, hostess and waitress.

I was told the handyman on the ranch and his wife were on the lam from the Houston police. I never got a straight answer from them when I asked why, but there was a rumor that he had been a pimp and that she was a call girl. At that time, I did not know what either of those terms meant but I did not want to appear dumb so I did not ask. They were very nice people, and good to me.

In addition to the horses, restaurant, and bar, the dude ranch had a swimming pool, a marina, and a private airstrip. When I was not busy learning ways to make money, I had the run of the facilities. I spent many happy hours that summer, earned enough to pay my tuition and buy books for my sophomore year at college, and learned a lot more about life than I had from my family. Someday, when all the guilty have departed for greener pastures, I may tell some of those stories.

33 - # 34 TOY STORE

Sales Lady and Lady Sales

While I was at the dude ranch, my older sister graduated from college. My parents told me I could go as an out–of-state student for my sophomore year in the fall of 1961. With dreams of the Colorado Rockies, I applied to the University of Colorado at Boulder. When the first of September arrived, I had not heard from them. I panicked, registered at the University of Texas and gave a deposit to a rooming house for young ladies. (Yes, young ladies. In the dark ages, college men and women were segregated. Women had a curfew and were locked up for the night!) This particular boarding house had the advantage of a separate garage apartment with an alley behind, large windows, and a deaf landlady. It seemed ideal to me.

About a week after registering at Texas, I received my acceptance to the University of Colorado. The delay was caused by a mail fire that had burned my health forms. The post office returned the charred remains to my doctor, who submitted a second set. Too late! I had already spent my money. I became a Texan as the result of a mail fire.

When I registered at Texas, I had to pick a major. My guidance counselor thought that, besides being a housewife and mother, there were only two careers available: teacher or nurse. That way I could adjust my schedule to be home with the kids. We tried teaching, remember? I chose nursing. The Introduction to Nursing class met at a local hospital where we were to assist the nurses. With no training and no experience, this meant we had to change bedpans and make beds. At the end of the first week, I returned to my guidance counselor to change my major. I did not want to be a teacher or a nurse. She insisted I could not be anything else. The standoff sent me to the dean's office, where I was told I could be a social worker. That became my next major.

My folks paid my room and board but I still needed a job. The university hired students but they paid only 25 cents an hour. A friend had a job at a toy store for the princely sum of a dollar an hour and he promised to speak to the owner on my behalf. Lucky me, I got the job. Unfortunately, it was too far from campus to walk, so I needed a car. I had $300.00 left from my summer job to use as a down payment on a new Volkswagen bug. With the job, I could make the payments.

My mother had a different idea. She paid a neighbor $300.00 for a 1949 Desoto, then told me I owed her the money. I was devastated and everyone at school made fun of my car. However, it did run. In fact, in cold weather, my car was the only car that would run. I must say, it made me feel good to offer rides to the snotty girls who looked down their noses at my chariot.

None of my roommates owned a car. Between school, work, and dating, I did not have time to drive around looking for parking, so they drove me. They drove me to and from school and work. In the meantime, they drove the car. I thought it was great, that is, until I realized I was spending all the money I earned on gas. When I complained, they convinced me the gas tank must have a leak. I paid good money to learn that the only leak was in the accelerator pedal. In nine months, they put 98,000 miles on the old baby and I needed a new car. Fortunately, I had been saving to buy the Volkswagen I originally wanted.

As to the job, I really liked working at the toy store. We carried many models of cars, planes, trains, etc., so the store was sort of a hangout for the pre-puberty set. When we were not busy selling stuff to their parents, we hung out with the kids. When no one else was in the store, we played with the toys. (Well, we did need to learn the stock.) The only time the boss objected was when we raced around the store shooting at each other with bazooka guns that used air pressure to shoot table tennis balls. He came through the door at just the wrong time and I accidentally hit him in a very sensitive place. I knew I was in trouble when he keeled over with a terrible grimace. I apologized profusely, promising never to do it again, so he did not fire me.

Another incident at the toy store brought me a different job offer of sorts. My boss's best friend was a high-powered attorney who drove a vintage Jaguar. Every time he came by the store, he flirted with me and told me I was too pretty to be working as a sales clerk. He told me he had connections at the Chicken Ranch. He was sure I could get a job there. Because of the Broadway play and a movie about the ranch, most of you have probable heard of the place. It was not make-believe—it really existed. For those of you who do not go to the movies or theaters, the Chicken Ranch was a popular "house of ill repute." I thought he was just bluffing, so one day I agreed. Imagine my shock when he brought the Madam to the toy store! She looked me up and down like a piece of meat, handed me her card, said, "Call me," and walked out of the store. I was speechless. I never called her, but I have often thought about the offer. I bet it paid better than a dollar an hour.

I worked at the toy store during the school term for two and a half years. The second year, with the new car payment, I went from part-time to full time. I made $37.50 a week, which I used to pay my rent, my car payment and to buy food, gas, and essentials. It seemed there was never any money left over. This is another life lesson. Over the years, I have had many jobs that paid much, much more. However, no matter how much I made, the take-home always paid for the same things. The size of the house and car got bigger, and the "essentials" a little fancier, but the end result was always the same. Working for someone else does keep a roof over your head, but you cannot work your way to riches as an employee.

35 OVERTIME

The new car meant new car payments, new car insurance and new car property tax. With the car, rent, food, tuition, books, etc., my $37.50 was a little short. I started looking for ways to make additional money.

The first thing I tried was overtime at the toy store. Now, people get paid time and a half for overtime work. Back then, no one had heard of such a ridiculous thing. If you worked hourly, you were paid the same thing for every hour you worked. Bosses were more willing to let employees work overtime because it did not cost them anything additional.

The downside to overtime is that there are just so many hours in a day. Fortunately, I was young, with lots of energy and little need to sleep. Even so, it was not too long before I realized that I had to find another way to make money.

36 TERM PAPERS

The next thing I tried was writing term papers. I wrote well and always got A's on my papers. One of my friends noticed this, and begged me to write her term paper for her. She told me she would fail out of school if she did not get a good grade and she did not think she could do a decent term paper.

I did not like the idea because it seemed dishonest, but she was a friend, so I wrote a paper for her. She was so pleased that she gave me $50.00 as a gift. I was delighted. When she told her sorority sisters that I had written her paper, my telephone rang off the hook. I cannot tell you how many people wanted me to do the same thing for them. Being honest, and chicken (I had images of being expelled), I declined. Besides, I do not like to write term papers. I told my potential customers about Cliff Notes, Classic Comic books, and the reference section of the library. I suggested they do their own papers the same way I did mine.

37 TYPING

The term paper deal made people aware of the fact that I had a typewriter and could type. This led to my next business venture: typing term papers. Most of the people who wanted me to do their papers could not type. When I told them how to do their papers, the inevitable response would be, "But I can't type" or "But I don't have a typewriter" and "Will you type it for me?"

This venture provided a steady source of income towards the end of each term. The downside was that I had to get my own term papers done early so I would have the time to type other people's papers. Also, I could not spell and typewriters had no spell-checker. I had to solve that problem to reduce complaints. People always say, "Use a dictionary." How do you look up a word in a dictionary if you cannot spell the word in the first place?

I worked a profit- sharing deal with my roommate. She corrected spelling, I typed, and she checked for typos. If I had been truly smart, I would have realized a business opportunity and started a company.

38 DEPOSITS

Back in the days before aluminum cans and recycling, stores charged a deposit for glass bottles, and cleaners charged for coat hangers. You got your money back when you returned the used item. If you really needed money for the niceties of life (such as food), this was a way to get instant cash.

Towards the end of the school year, my roommate and I would prowl the alleys and byways around campus, collecting bottles and coat hangers. People tend to get suspicious when you start poking in their garbage, but we looked like wholesome kids, so we never ran into trouble.

This is certainly NOT a method for an individual to get rich, either quickly or slowly. However, it works to generate immediate income in a pinch. It also works great as a fundraiser for non-profit groups. The next time your organization puts on a fair or festival, set up collection points for the aluminum cans and advertise that the profits from sale goes to benefit your cause. The last time I proposed this for a group, they made $54,000.00 from the effort.

39 FACTORY WORK

This one did not work for me, but it does for many people, so it is worth mentioning. When I was little, Mom read me a story about a mouse who dawdled so he was always late coming home. One day, his family moved off and left him. The rest of the story is about his search for his family. Since I am perpetually late, I worried that one day I would come home to find my family gone.

During my sophomore year in college, my family moved from Houston to Dallas, Texas. When I went home for Christmas, it was to a motel. I got lost and had to drive around looking for it. By spring, they had moved into a rental house and I had to repeat the experience of finding my family. This brought me uncomfortably close to the story of the mouse. Instead of working at the dude ranch I resolved to return home for the summer.

The want ads for Dallas revealed an interesting fact: Dallas had a lot of manufacturing companies. Work at a factory paid better than other jobs and night work paid even more. Off I went to apply. The first place I tried manufactured circuit boards. The application process involved filling out the application and taking a written test, followed by an interview and a practical exam.

For the better part of the day, I moved from room to room, passing each phase (and of course not telling them I would be leaving in the fall.) When I finally got to the practical part, I was ushered into a room with two women who were also taking the test. They were wearing dresses made from feed sacks and to my college student eye, they looked like they had just been released from a home for the mentally challenged.

The practical test involved placing ten differently-shaped wooden blocks into a board with matching shapes (stars, squares, circles, etc.) It looked exactly like a Mattel toy we sold at the toy store. I was elated. I thought for sure I would get the job! The man running the test set a timer and told us to start. In a blitz of activity, the two feed sacks finished their boards. When the timer sounded, I was still trying to figure out where the third block went. The man frowned at my board and told the other two they could leave. When the door closed, he said, "Listen, you made the highest grade on our written test that anyone has ever made. I want to give you another chance." This time, I made it to the fourth block before the timer sounded. The man gave me a look of disgust as I rejoined the smiling feed sacks to proceed to the next section of the test.

This was to see if you could thread a needle while looking through a microscope. The set-up required the use of your right hand. Not only am I left-handed, but I wore glasses. The flower sacks had the needle threaded while I was still trying to find the needle through the lens. The man asked them to leave and said the same thing to me that the other man said.

I explained that I was left-handed and that I thought that might be why I failed. He brightened and said they had an opening on their left-handed line. He ushered me to the left-hand setup and I tried, and tried, and tried again. This time, I could see the needle, but I could not get the thread lined up with the hole. The man shook his head sadly and I returned to the waiting room. After a while, a man came to announce that the feed sacks were hired and I could go home.

Embarrassed and dejected, I was forced to reevaluate my opinion of the women in the feed sack dresses. They could do something I could not.

What I learned from this experience was that physical appearance and test scores do not necessarily translate into the ability to do the job. Different jobs require different skills. I also learned not to apply for jobs that require hand and eye coordination, because I have none.

40 SHOE STORE

After many, many applications, I finally landed a job as a shoe salesman in Dallas at a store run by a couple. This time, I got the job because of my physical appearance. The man had a roving eye and the wife a jealous temper. She did not like me from the first moment our eyes met. I thought it would not be a problem, because I certainly had no interest in him. I took the job because it paid salary plus commission and because he hired me. I figured I could smile at her, stay away from him, and get paid until school started.

I did not think about the fact the shoe store had a large back room with a maze of shoe racks. In addition, I certainly did not think he would have the nerve to accost me in the back room with his wife on the show room floor. WRONG! I spent three miserable weeks smiling at her, dodging him, and trying to figure out how I could return to school if I quit this miserable job.

Fortunately, the dude ranch called and asked me to return. I skipped off to paradise for the rest of the summer.

41 - # 42 YELLOWSTONE PARK

Salary and Tips

Having learned my lesson about minimum wage summer jobs in town, in 1963 I did what I think every young person should do, work at a National Park. I was lucky to get a job at Yellowstone National Park. Back then the National Park Service contracted with vendors to run the hotels, restaurants, and concessions. Parks open only for the summer, such as Yellowstone, hired college kids. Imagine being paid to live in a premiere tourist attraction for three months with a crowd of kids your own age!

Most jobs provided room, board, and a small salary. If you were lucky and got a job as a waitress, busboy, bartender, or maid, you also got tips. Tips are definitely the way to go unless you are like my friend Kay, who received a cancelled two-cent stamp as a tip.

I worked as a waitress in the main dining room at Canyon Lake Lodge. As the only restaurant in that part of the park, we never lacked for customers. While kids with other jobs made less than minimum wage ($1.25 an hour) I made what they did plus $50 to $100 a day in tips, which was for those days fantastic.

We worked rotating shifts of two meals a day, six days a week. That meant we always had part of the day off to see the sights or party. On days that I worked lunch and dinner, I got to sleep late. If I worked breakfast and lunch the day before my day off, then lunch and dinner the day after my day off, I got off two days. If I got bored with Yellowstone, I could go places like Sun Valley or The Grand Tetons.

Waitresses were supposed to give busboys ten per cent of their tips. Most of the girls did not want to share, so they lied about how much they received. I did not think that was fair. Because I shared my tips fairly, the busboys give me preferential service.

After the first week, I noticed two things: 1) the bus boys cleared the tables and knew how much the tips were. The girls who cheated soon had trouble getting their tables cleared at all. 2) If tables were cleared quickly, more customers could be served and more money made.

Some of the boys were especially helpful, so I gave them more than 10%. This resulted in even more help from more people. They not only cleared and set up my tables before others, but they also did some of my work, such as filling water glasses, bring bread and butter, etc. This resulted in better service for my customers and higher tips for us.

The fact that I provided better service to more customers did not escape management's attention. I was praised for my work. The fact that I received more help, more money, and more praise did not escape the attention of the other girls. What they did not understand was how I did it. I told them my formula for success: "Share the tips fairly and reward the behavior you want."

32 girls worked in the dining room. Only one understood what I said and put it into practice. Soon there were two of us receiving more help, more money, and more praise. The other 31 complained to the manager saying it was not fair that the busboys help us more than they helped them. The manager asked the boys, "Is this true?" They explained that we shared tips fairly and paid extra for extra service, while the others cheated them. Of course, they cleared our tables first and helped any way they could.

The manager told the girls to follow our example. Do you know none of them did? Instead, they tried to convince us that we should do as they did!

43 COINS

Because I did not have money for tuition, I left college at the midpoint of my senior year. (Yes, there is a story about what happened to the money I made in Yellowstone, but this story is about how to make money, not how to spend it. The other story will have to wait another day.)

I brought back 40 silver dollars from Yellowstone that I saved until the end of the semester when I badly needed some money. I deposited the silver dollars in my checking account. The bank teller seemed ecstatic at my deposit, but I did not understand why. Later, I learned that the Federal Government had released some old silver coins near Yellowstone Park.

When I made the $40 deposit, the coins were worth about eight dollars apiece. That $320 would have paid my tuition so I could have stayed in school. I did not make money from the coins, but I bet the bank teller did. I mention it to you now, so you do not make the same mistake. Check the value of any old or unusual coins that come your way.

44 VOLUNTEER WORK

Before I move past my college years, I wanted to include a couple of paragraphs about a volunteer experience I had in college that helped set the stage for latter success.

My sophomore year in college, I was selected chairman of a Student Union committee. There were two decorating committees: the Regular Decorations Committee and the Special Decorations Committee. I was chair of the Special Decorations Committee and another girl was chair of the Regular Decorations Committee. Each of us had twelve people on our committee. I could not get the 12 assigned people to do anything. My close friends and I did all work. We got the job done, but it was no fun. (I never want to make another Kleenex carnation again in my life!)

Whenever work needed to be done, the Regular Decorations Chairperson always had at least 50 people volunteering to help. Every time I saw her in action, I wondered, "How does she do that? How does she get people to work for her?" It took me a number of years to learn how to get people to work for me, but I did learn. Stay tuned for a later episode in this secret to business success.

In the meantime, if there is some career you would like to pursue, but do not have the background, try volunteer work. You will learn about your area of interest and gain experience that might help you find the job of your dreams.

45 - # 48 SHARPSTOWN STATE BANK

Bookkeeping, Head Cashier, Teller, Loan Officer

By 1964 my family had moved back to Houston, Texas. Since I did not have the money for tuition, I returned home. My first job after college was with Sharpstown State Bank.

Old timers may remember Sharpstown because in 1971 the Federal Government filed a lawsuit against Frank Sharp, the owner of the bank. This prompted a depositors' run on the bank, forcing its closure in what was then the biggest bank failure in the history of the Federal Deposit Insurance Corporation. (Bank closures are old news now, but then it was a big deal. For the full story, Google "Sharpstown Scandal.")

The bank was in a five-story building attached to a shopping center and the upper floors were leased as office space. My original plan was to work there long enough to get the money to go back to school. But of course, I did not tell them that. As it worked out, that is not what happened anyway.

Looking for a real job was a very discouraging adventure. I had three and a half years of college. That meant I was over- or under-qualified for almost everything. My college major was social work, but remember, that was only because I did not want to be a schoolteacher or nurse. I filled out applications, but most social work jobs required at least a B.A. if not a master's. When I applied for jobs that required only a high school diploma, they would tell me that I was over-educated and would not stay. In desperation, I applied for anything and everything and pleaded my case. The banker that finally hired me said: "I'm probably making a mistake because you won't stay," but he was willing to give me a chance. (His mistake, he was right, I did not stay!)

My banking career began in bookkeeping where my job was to sort checks in alphabetical order. As you can imagine, this was very challenging work. The challenge was to stay awake. My co-workers were young mothers. Because we got off at 2:30 this was a perfect job for them. There was plenty of time to pick up the kids from day care and get home to fix dinner. Most of the time was spent gossiping about husbands, kids, friends, neighbors, bosses, and fellow workers. My problem was I had no kids, no husband, and no interest in gossip. Therefore, I worked.

On my first day on the job, I finished my share of the checks two hours after I arrived. Since I hate to sit with nothing to do, I asked the head cashier for more work. The only male in bookkeeping, he was a nervous young man who could not handle anything out of the ordinary and did not know how to deal with the women under him. To have someone ask for more work was certainly out of the ordinary.

After some hemming and hawing, he suggested I help the other girls. They were only too happy to pass their checks to me. Then one by one, they disappeared into the ladies' restroom. Before long, I was sorting checks all by myself. By noon, I had finished the lot and went looking for more work. What I found were numerous odd jobs, like filing signature cards and ledgers, purging old files, etc.

Although the head cashier sat in the same room with us, this went on for several days before the he noticed that I was the only one working. When he asked me where everyone was, I told him they were in the restroom. Embarrassed, he turned bright red and pulled at his collar. He stammered for a while and finally said, "Will you go into the restroom and inquire how long they planned to remain there?"

I told the girls that the head cashier wanted to know when they would return to their desks. They told me to tell him they would come out when they were finished. I guess they did not finish until time to go home, because they did not come out until then. The same thing happened for the rest of the week.

By the end of my first week, I realized several things. First, there was not enough work to keep us all busy. In fact, there was not enough work to keep me busy! Next, if I continued to do all the work, the other girls would eventually be fired, and I did not want that to happen. Third, our manager did not know how to manage and was intimidated by the crowd of girls. I decided to slow down and visit like the other girls. I spent the next week learning about my fellow workers and doing as little work as possible (for me, anyway.) I had been taught to deliver a day's work for a day's wages and I felt guilty if I did not work while being paid. Obviously, my fellow workers did not share this view. In fact, they believed they were not being paid enough for the work they did. Therefore, they did as little as possible.

Most of them did not need to work. Their husbands paid all the bills. They worked so they could have spending money, or at least that is what they told me. The unofficial leader of the group had three children. Most of her conversation was about problems and expenses with daycare and how hard it was to find a good maid. She always borrowed lunch or bus money, complaining about the low pay and her lack of money.

After listening to her for several days, I realized that she was spending more money to work than she was making. I showed her the figures and thought she would be pleased when I explained that she would have more money if she stayed home. Boy, was I naive! She huffed up, informed me that she liked to work, and stormed off to the rest room. She told the others that I had said something hateful to her, and for a while none of them would talk to me.

For the next three weeks, the routine continued. I worked as slowly as possible, did most of the sorting and went to the restroom to check on the rest of the girls when the head cashier requested. When I finished sorting checks, I looked around for other things that needed doing. On Monday of the fourth week I was asked to go to the bank president's office. I was nervous, sure that I would be fired for doing so little work. Instead, he promoted me to head cashier with a $50.00 a week raise. What a surprise! I told him I wanted the job, but was not sure I knew enough. He said, "Yes you do, you know how to get the #*!*# girls out of the bathroom.' The former head cashier happily returned to the teller window.

The first week of my reign over bookkeeping was a little rocky. By this time, the girls were used to having someone else (me) do their work, and spent most of their time in the restroom reading books and talking. On day one of my take over, I passed out the checks to sort equally among the girls and told them that when they finished their stack, they were to report to me for additional work. When one of them disappeared into the restroom, I checked the clock. After 20 minutes, I went to the restroom to request she return to her desk. I had to retrieve the leader of the pack eight times the first day. As each girl finished her stack, I assigned new work.

Aside from supervising the staff, the head cashier was responsible for keeping reports. In this bank, that meant I got slips of paper from each teller and from the note department. I totaled these and turned the results in to the bank president. By the end of the week, I had mastered my meager responsibilities as head cashier. The staff was somewhat sullen, but the bookkeeping department was totally in order, clean and current. There were no more odd jobs I could assign to keep the girls busy.

Over the weekend, I developed a plan of action. Monday morning, I showed up with baked goods and informed the girls that we would have a staff meeting. I started by explaining that there was not enough work to keep everyone busy. I was afraid management might let some of us go if they found out (the stick.) I said that our job was to get the work done, but that it was also to look busy, so none of us would lose our job (the carrot.) I asked each girl to write down on a piece of paper how much time it really took to finish her assigned job. I totaled the time estimates and divided by the number of work hours in a day. The results indicated that only three people were needed to do the job seven of us were hired to do (confirmation of the stick.) Everyone in the room looked stricken.

Next, I mentioned some of the odd jobs like filing ledgers that we could do to look busy and I asked for suggestions. I was amazed! They not only included all the tasks I knew needed doing, but they also suggested cleaning, dusting, washing, and decorating. Between us, we made a list of additional tasks and times and each girl agreed to accept additional assignments. This brought the estimate of needed employees to four. More worried looks.

I mentioned that not everyone showed up to work every day and suggested we give back- up assignments. This would pad our hours. The girls readily agreed. Finally, I suggested longer breaks and lunches, with the caveat that no more than three girls should be absent at the same time and no one should divulge our secret. If anyone asked where someone was, they were to be told that the person was on an errand to the note department or to a teller window. That way, if management came to bookkeeping, we would always look busy.

The meeting accomplished much more than I expected and a little more than I wanted. I left with a new back-up assistant, the leader of the pack. Since there was not enough work to keep me busy I was somewhat reluctant to share. However, what could I do? If I wanted the girls to buy into the program, I had to go along. It took me about half a day to teach my new assistant the routine. After that she was doing all my work and I was back looking for something to do.

Within a week, the change in the bookkeeping department was evident to everyone in the bank. The place was a beehive of apparent activity, we were current on everything, and the place was sparkling clean and decorated. The girls had extended the decorations to include other parts of the bank and had assigned themselves to bring in baked goods every day. This meant that other bank employees spent a good deal of time hanging around, so the room looked full even when my girls were out on their extra breaks.

My assistant proved better at dealing with any personnel problems that cropped up than I was, so I gave her that job too. She loved it. This left me with nothing to do but listen to her reports and turn in the final report to the bank president.

One benefit the bank offered was to pay for banking courses for any employee who asked. Since I had literally nothing to do, I signed up. For the next three months, I spent my time studying banking. Using what I learned, I developed a ledger sheet and set of reports.

Instead of receiving scraps of paper with amounts from employees of other departments, I had them enter the amounts in the ledger and initial. This saved copying bad handwriting and established accountability.

Next, I developed a set of reports. Since my assistant no longer had to re-copy data, she wanted something to do to look busy too. I assigned her to total the data and type the reports. This impressed the boss, and I was promoted to the teller window and given another $50.00 raise. My assistant got the head cashier job and a raise. She made me promise I would not reveal the secret about looking busy. I promised.

Security at the bank appeared impressive. In the morning tellers lined up flanked by security guards while a bank officer opened the vault. Tellers paraded in one at a time, checked out a money box, counted the cash, and got back in line. When the last teller got a box, the parade moved to bookkeeping to report the cash total of the assigned box. When this ritual was completed, the security guards marched the line of tellers to their stations. At each station, while the rest of the tellers stood at attention, the assigned teller unlocked the cash drawer, installed the box, and locked the drawer.

The two drive-in windows were separate from the main bank and reached by an underground tunnel that dead-ended under the booths. A security guard would hold the cash box while the teller crawled up the ladder into the booth. The guard would then hand the box to the teller. When the last teller was installed, the guards returned to the main bank to patrol the premises.

At the end of the day, each teller balanced the receipts and checks and counted the cash in their box. The security guards arrived to retrieve the tellers and their boxes. The teller parade reformed window at a time to retrace the steps through bookkeeping to the vault.

My first visit to the vault was to witness this process. As the tellers counted their money, I had time to look around and wonder. As I passed into the vault, I was impressed by the size and thickness of the vault door and by how quiet the vault was. The cash boxes were kept in a separate room off the main vault. The door to the room was a regular wooden door, inset into the thick vault walls. I wondered why I could hear noise from the Note Department in this room, but not in the main vault. I also wondered why the teller windows each carried about $70, 000, when I knew from bookkeeping that the usual day's business was less than $10,000 per window. These questions would be answered later.

My first week as a teller, I was assigned to relief. This meant I took over the window while the assigned teller went on break. Between breaks, I sat with different tellers as they explained the job. Since I did not have an assigned window, I had no cash box but shared the box with the resident teller. This fact probably keep me out of Leavenworth and saved my job.

Initially, I was excited about learning something new. However, after an hour in the window, I realized the teller job was actually less complicated than bookkeeping. If you could count, read, write, and talk to people, you had it made. (Remember the Dark Ages, before computers?) Most of the time was spent waiting for customers. The trick was to remember the customers and their accounts. Because all records were on paper, you had to call, or go to bookkeeping to check accounts.

When the regular teller left for lunch, I felt ready to take on the world. Before I took over the window, I asked the teller if I should count the bills or the bundles of cash. He said, "Oh, just count the bundles." Since I enjoyed counting my own money, I thought I would enjoy playing with the bank money. However I learned, when it belongs to someone else, it is just dirty paper. And I mean really dirty. I could hardly wait to wash my hands after handling the mess.

My first customer was a man who would not make eye contact. I felt uncomfortable as he stood in front of my window and wrote his check. I felt even more uncomfortable when I looked at the check. It was for $65,000 and was written against an account that had been overdrawn the last time I looked. What I remembered about that particular account was a series of large deposits and withdrawals, more of the latter than the former. I excused myself to retreat to bookkeeping to check the account. About half way there, I noticed all the other tellers had stopped working and were staring at me. The former head bookkeeper moved toward me, waiving me back and mouthing "NO, NO." In a stage whisper, I said, "But, I don't think this check is any good!"

When I said that, he grabbed my arm and pulled me through the doors into bookkeeping. He told me the man at my window was Frank Sharp, the bank owner, and that I was to cash his check no matter what. I argued that the account had no money and showed him the ledger sheet. He explained that it did not matter and said, "If you want to keep your job, you had better give him the money." I told him that I would not release the money unless he OK'd the check. He signed, not me. Later that week, a deposit was received to cover the withdrawal.

Several years later when Frank Sharp was arrested, one of the charges was kiting checks. This works by having multiple bank accounts. You write a bad check on Account A as a deposit to Account B, then withdraw the money from Account B. Next you deposit a check from Account B to Account A to cover the original bad check. If you really got into it, you could add Bank C, D, E, etc., until you spent the whole day running around town, depositing and cashing checks. To protect themselves against this process, most banks now require a lag time between deposit and withdrawal for large sums. However, at the time it was a useful tool for high rollers who needed funds for a short time. I finally realized the reason the teller windows carried so much cash was to be available for Frank Sharp's use with no fuss or bother.

Days 2, 3, and 4 of my teller ship were routine and convinced me I would have lots of opportunity to study my banking courses. I did enjoy visiting with customers, though, and all in all, it was a better way to spend the day than in bookkeeping.

Day 5 brought its own terror. At lunch, one of the drive-in tellers went home sick. They sent me to take over her window for the rest of the day. Since she departed in a hurry, the guard was waiting at the booth with the cash box. I climbed in and counted the bundles while he watched.

About an hour later, I noticed I needed one-dollar bills. I called to request permission to buy some ones and used a bundle of hundreds to pay for the bills. This was a normal transaction. What was not normal was when the inside teller called me to tell me that a hundred-dollar bill was missing from the bundle. Oops! The security guards arrived to close down my widow and count the money—the real bills, not just the bundles. Two more $100 bundles were missing a bill each for a total of $300.00 missing on my watch. That was more than I earned in a month. I thought for sure, at best, I would have to make up the money; at worst, they would drag me off to jail, but neither happened.

What did happen was a complete investigation -- the police, bank examiners, a lie detector test, and, finally, the FBI. I was cleared from suspicion because I passed the lie detector test and because the guard testified that I only counted the bundles, not the bills. They never charge anyone with the theft because they determined that seven people, including the guard and me, had access to the cash drawer. Most of the suspicion fell on the regular teller, who was later arrested for kiting checks. I thanked God when the investigation was over, and never, ever took over another window without counting all the bills. Three months later I was given another $50.00 raise and promoted to the Note Department as a loan officer.

I found working in the Note Department to be very interesting. I also learned a lot about financial markets and mortgage paper. The Note Department was on the other side of the vault from bookkeeping. If you remember, noise from the Note Department could be heard in the vault. I soon realized that noise in the vault could be heard in the Note Department. This raised my curiosity enough to investigate. What I learned was that only a sheet rock wall separated the room with the cash boxes from the Note Department. At some time, someone cut a door in the vault wall and added a room to the side. Why this was done, I could only speculate.

This speculation took on a sinister tone when I realized that behind the vault there was a stairwell, used to store paper, envelopes, and other bank supplies. My curiosity led me to walk up the stairs, which went up to the fifth floor with openings on every floor. To rob the bank, all one had to do was wait until the bank closed, then go to an upper floor of the shopping center, walk down into the bank and knock a hole in the sheet rock wall! To test this theory, at lunch, I went to the shopping center. Sure enough, the stairwell was not locked. Considering the eventual demise of the bank, I wonder if it was set up that way on purpose.

My banking career was short lived, because in one week, I got two job offers that changed the direction of my financial future. The first offer was from Eastern Airlines. I was offered a job as a stewardess based out of Miami, Florida. This job paid about the same as the bank job, but had the added advantage of glamour and travel. The other offer was from the Texas Department of Public Welfare. (Remember my college major?) The job paid twice as much as the bank job. At the time, it seemed like a veritable fortune.

What should I do? Should I go for the glamour or for the money? I decided to go for the glamour. I figured I was young, and the money would come later. Several things happened to change that decision. When I told my mother I was planning to take the airline job, rather than return to school, she told me I would have to pay rent. I was seriously dating a graduate student at that time. He was upset when I told him about the job offers, my decision to accept the airline job, and my mother's proclamation. His reaction surprised me. His response was, "Well, if you have to pay rent there, we might as well get married." So, I took the social worker job and got married.

When I told the bank president that I planned to leave, he told me I should stay, that I had a great future in banking. In retrospect, he was probably right. However, by leaving when I did, I missed the closing of the bank by the State and Federal bank regulators and the arrest of the owner and some of the other bank officials. I am not sure how that would looked on my resume. I am just glad that I did not have to deal with it.

49 SOCIAL WORKER

The job with the Texas State Department of Public Welfare turned out to be my first real career and could be a book by itself. I worked for them from 1964 to 1980. Since the purpose of this book is to discuss ways to make money, not ways to live without it, I will just hit a few highlights. I was 20 years old and very excited. A social worker, me, a social worker! The first month on the job I was sent from Houston to Austin, Texas for training

After training, I reported to my Houston supervisor, a crusty old man who said, "I did not want to hire you. You are too young. You'll get married and leave me as soon as I get you broken in where you can be of some use to me." I asked, "If you feel that way why did you hired me?" He said, "I had no choice. My boss insisted."

Since I did not know anyone who worked for the Welfare Department, I was curious. It turned out his boss was the woman who interviewed me the previous year. She had been very complimentary and had implied that I would get the job. Later she called to apologize and said, "They hired an older woman." The older woman turned out to be the daughter of a friend of the local welfare director. She was one month older than me. I had been her first choice, but politics dictated she hire someone else. The fact that her authority had been usurped caused her to go to bat for me when the next job came available.

This time politics worked for me and I learned a lesson about government employment: Things happen because individuals want them to. If you want a government job, never underestimate the role of politics. There may be tests, lists, and civil service procedures galore, but in the end, the people in charge hire and promote whomever they want, for whatever reason they want.

In 1964, I was the youngest person employed as a caseworker in Houston, Texas. Most of my clients were in "old folks' homes," the name used for nursing homes before Medicare and Medicaid. I will never forget my first week. Since I was the new kid on the block, everyone dumped problem cases on me. I was shocked by the deplorable living conditions some people were forced to endure, the number of characters I encountered, and the revelation that octogenarians actually expected me, ME, a 20-year-old kid, to address their financial, medical and emotional problems! In the following examples, I've changed names to protect the guilty.

My first home visit was to a dilapidated old mansion that could easily serve as the setting for a Halloween horror show. The building looked and smelled like it should be condemned. It was badly in need of paint and most of the shutters hung at odd angles. Except for the skeletal people perched around the porch, I would have thought the place was deserted.

I mounted the steps and asked the skeletons if the owner was in. One of them shuffled off to find her. The others gathered around and asked, "Are you the new Welfare Lady?" When I told them "Yes," someone asked "Who did you come to see?" I told them the name of the double amputee I was scheduled to visit. They laughed. Since I had received the same response from my co-workers, I asked, "Why are you laughing?" They all said, "You'll see."

Before long, the owner of the home came shuffling through the torn screen door. She wore oversized fluffy house shoes and looked almost as old as the skeletons on the porch. She was, however, fat. I told her whom I wanted to see. She cackled as she led me through the maze that was this old folks' home. When I asked why she had laughed, she replied, "You'll see."

I followed her up to the second, then to the third floor. On the third floor she stopped and pointed to a narrow stairwell up to the attic. The stairs were so steep they resembled a ladder. By this point, my apprehension was extremely high, but I entered the stairwell anyway. As my body blocked the light from the room behind, all I could see was a bare light bulb hanging overhead surrounded by darkness. The stink of urine increased as my nose rose, step by step.

When my head cleared the landing I shifted my gaze from the ceiling to the room. Blinking, as my eyes adjusted to the dim light, I saw a form, backlit by the bare bulb and sitting in a straight-backed wooden chair. Another couple of blinks brought the figure more in focus. I could see three bare leg stumps, hanging off the front edge of the wooden chair. This must be my double amputee, I thought. OOPS! – Three?! Imagine my chagrin when I realized I was not staring at three bare leg stumps but two bare leg stumps and a penis. It seems my double amputee did not like to wear pants, any pants. After the initial shock, I shifted my gaze to his face and finished my ascent to the attic.

I found a totally non-judgmental place in my mind and spent the next half-hour avoiding looking at anything except his face, which was covered by a lewd grin. At the interview's end, I could hardly wait to get out of that attic and away from that old folks' home, but I seemed to have passed some kind of test. The operator of the home passed the word to the other homes that I was OK. After that, my fellow workers and the operators let me know what I was getting into before I climbed the stairs. This ability to move into non-judgmental reactions and to use selective focus has served me well over the years. My regret is that I do not do it all the time.

Another welfare story is about a woman I will call Mary, who was in her eighties. Originally from Ireland, she had a wonderful Irish accent, wore a hat and gloves, and carried a parasol. She looked like a storybook grandmother and was the sweetest, dearest little old lady without a single relative in the world. She was too sick to live on her own but too well for a nursing home. At that time, the maximum old age assistance check was $83 per month. Nursing homes cost $300-$500 per month. Without a nursing care supplement, it was extremely difficult to find care for people in Mary's situation. (It still is.) Most of them ended up in the worst of the old folks' homes or in rundown boarding houses where operators took all of their pension checks.

I met Mary when she appeared at my desk, suitcase in hand, and informed me that I was to pay for the taxi that brought her to my office. Fool that I was, I went to the curb and paid the man. When I returned, Mary told me she had a misunderstanding with the operator of the home where she lived and that I was to find her a new place to stay. She said, "I plan to camp out in your office until you find me somewhere to live." I called the home and confirmed that the operator was upset and did not want her back. Mary had taken other taxicabs and had told the driver to collect from the home's operator. (Sound familiar?) From Mary's perspective, she had no option. She gave the home all her money, didn't she? I got on the telephone and started looking for a home.

To my surprise, one of the most expensive nursing homes in town agreed to take her. Run by a non-profit group, the tab included transportation and activities, so I thought that might solve the taxi problem. Mary lasted there nearly two months before she showed up on my doorstep again. This time, the problem was food. Mary took the nursing home shuttle to the grocery store where she charged what she wanted to the home. The irate operator told me that it started with tea and cookies. Mary wanted tea time. At first they thought it was kind of cute and a good idea, so they started serving tea and cookies to all the residents. Then Mary expanded the menu to include extra items for lunch and dinner. Since she was buying things for all the residents, the operator did not say anything. The final straw was when the cook threatened to quit if Mary was not kept out of the kitchen. Mary had been hungry for some boiled beef and had a beef carcass delivered to the kitchen. According to the cook, it looked and smelled like road kill. Enough! Mary had to go and I had to find her a new place to live.

Over the next several months, the story repeated itself with variations. I did everything for Mary except take her home with me. I finally found a boardinghouse near her church that would let her keep part of her check as spending money. That seemed to do the trick as first one month passed, than another, without a taxi delivering Mary to my desk. I heaved a sigh of relief and moved on to other people and other problems.

Then one day I got a call from the boarding house operator. Mary and her suitcase had disappeared. Somewhat worried, I called a lady from her church. When I told her Mary had disappeared, she laughed and said, "Mary has not disappeared. She has taken her yearly trip to

Europe!" She told me not to worry, assuring me that Mary would be back at my office in the fall.

Sure enough, come fall, Mary walked in my door looking for a place to stay. When I asked her how she managed the trip, she explained that she got a berth on a working ship. She loaded a basket with bread, cheese, wine, and other stuff so she would not have the expense of food. Once in Europe, she had friends with whom she stayed. As to how she bought the ticket, did I not remember that she sold a national church magazine? Her record showed she had told all her social workers, including me, about the church magazine she sold. None of us thought she could make much money selling it and had never asked. Boy, where we wrong! Her tax returns showed she was doing quite well!

I learned a lot from Mary. First, do not assume anything about any client. Before you try to help someone, check into their own resources. Most people can care for themselves and their needs. Ask questions, make suggestions, but let people help themselves when they can. Next, check first. Some things that do not appear to make money can. The last thing I learned was, if you want it enough, you can figure out a way to get what you want. The next time you think you can't do something because you don't have the money, remember Mary. If an octogenarian in poor health and on welfare can figure out how to get to Europe, you can too!

As the majority of my clients were in nursing homes, I quickly learned that most patients were too medicated or out of it to know I was in the room. For these patients, the job was to check the home records and track down family members, if any. I learned that most nursing home residents had family, but few had family that spent any time at the home. There were a few patients who always had company. These relatives were an excellent source of information about the conditions in the home. All had horror stories to relate, and felt that their presence helped their relatives receive better care. However, all were afraid to say anything publicly because of fear of retribution.

I saw that when a patient had regular company, the quality of care improved, as did the quality of life. My dream was to create an organization similar to the Parent-Teacher Association (PTA) used by schools to encourage the involvement of families. I called my dream organization the PCA, the Patient Care Association. The idea was to organize patients' relatives into a support group for themselves and to improve the quality of life for people in institutional settings by providing increased participation by relatives and power through union.

Because the State Welfare assigned caseworkers to every home and had records of families for most patients in the homes, I imagined a state-sponsored effort to create the PCA. Social workers could organize the local chapters. Unfortunately, my boss just thought I was crazy. Later in my career, I served on a committee to look into ways to improve the quality of life for patients in nursing homes. Although this would be a low-cost effort, I could not convince the members of the committee to recommend the program. I still think it is a good idea; maybe someone who reads this can establish a grant to form such an organization.

For patients who were mentally alert, about one or two out of ten, the pressing need was for company, for someone to listen. I learned to balance my home visits to allow time to visit. My regret now is that I did not record the conversations. I had interviews with people born into slavery and many who remembered the aftermath of the Civil War. I heard stories of crossing the country in a covered wagon, of life on the prairie in a sod home, of cowboys and Indians and Texas Rangers. I listened to people who rode with Poncho Villa and who ran from Poncho Villa, to veterans who charged up San Juan Hill with Teddy Roosevelt and survived the Spanish American War, and to survivors of the Holocaust and two world wars, including the Bataan Death March.

Mentally, I accompanied a family as they escaped to freedom, surviving the Nazis only to have their country taken over by the Communists. I spend one afternoon with an elderly brother and sister who survived the 1900 Galveston hurricane. The roof of their house blew off and turned over. Their father plucked them from the water and threw them in the roof and they sailed across the island. Another afternoon, a widow recounted the Texas City disaster, an industrial accident that occurred April 16, 1947, in the port of Texas City; it was the deadliest industrial accident in U.S. history and triggered the first class-action lawsuit against the United States government. I listened to stories of Dust Bowl days where families lost their homes and their hope, rode the rails, and traveled to California in search of jobs. I heard firsthand accounts of the last hundred years. These conversations made history come alive. Incidents like the Civil War that seem ancient history to me before suddenly became real and relevant. I've often thought that schools should set up a program to bring elderly people to schools to lecture, or bring the kids to the nursing homes to hear the history of the recent and not-so-recent past.

When I married, I moved to Galveston, Texas and transferred to the Galveston welfare office. For the next couple of years, I worked with blind and disabled people and with the Aid to Families with Dependent Children program, as well as with some old age assistance recipients in nursing homes. The stories I heard could fill several books, but not this one.

50 NON-PROFITS

If what you want to do can be structured as a non-profit corporation, you benefit not only by not having to pay taxes on the money you raise, but can also quality for contributions, grants and some low-interest loans. "Non-profit" does not mean you cannot make money; it is a taxing authority designation that places limits on how the money made can be spent to maintain the tax-deductible nature of the money earned. Salaries can be paid. Blue Cross/Blue Shield is a non-profit corporation; so are the Red Cross and all churches.

While daydreaming about how the world would be if it were perfect for me, I have had a number of ideas for creating non-profit companies. For several of these, I worked out full-blown business plans, but due to time constraints, never put them into effect.

Some of the ideas I shared with friends who did put them into effect. For example, a friend of mine wanted to create co-op housing for low-income people. I helped her by creating a project and a plan. First, she formed a non-profit corporation, then she received a huge grant to set up a co-op program for residents in public housing.

Next, she got property management contracts with private apartment owners in low-income areas and organized the residents into management co-ops. The last time I talked to her, she had received a grant from the National Co-op Bank to create co-operative housing units. She and her staff were busy buying up apartment buildings to convert to co-ops. Some of my other ideas I may yet put into practice.

51 JOHN SEALY HOSPITAL

Director of Hospital Based Welfare Office

In 1967, when I was 25, Medicare and Medicaid were enacted. In Texas, the State Department of Public Welfare was assigned responsibility for implementing the Medicaid program. At that time John Sealy Hospital, associated with the University of Texas Medical School in Galveston, was the only state-supported hospital in Texas. Therefore, indigents (i.e., poor people) with major medical problems, congregated in Galveston. In an attempt to maximize federal funding, the hospital requested that the State Welfare Department establish a hospital-based office to process applications for welfare assistance, including Medicare and Medicaid. Because of my connection to the hospital (my husband, the medical student) I was asked if I would like to work at the hospital. I said, "Yes." The office was to be the first hospital-based welfare office in the nation.

The inception was rather rough. My boss arranged for a meeting with the hospital administrative staff. The day before the meeting I received a State of Texas Medicaid Policy Manual and a copy of the Medicare regulations. Everyone in the office received the same documents.

The day of the meeting all the bigwigs from the state capital arrived. The procession into the meeting lasted longer than the presentation to the hospital staff. The hospital president, Dr. Truman Graves Blocker, Jr., who was also dean of the medical school, introduced our Commissioner of Welfare. The commissioner made a short speech about the momentous nature of the Medicare/ Medicaid legislation. He explained that the office we would establish was the first of its kind in the nation. He introduced me as the Medicare/Medicaid EXPERT who would establish and direct the office and then he left, not just the podium, but the room.

All the welfare dignitaries jumped up and hurried out of the room after the commissioner. When I tried to follow, my boss's boss said, "No. You stay and explain to the hospital staff what you plan to do." I was terror-stricken! No one told me I needed to prepare a speech, much less a plan! No one told me I was to set up an office, much less to be the director! I thought I would do the same thing I had been doing all along, social work. As my boss turned to leave, I grabbed his coat sleeve, pleaded with him not to leave me, and asked what I was to do. His response was, "I do not know. We'll think of something." Then he left.

When I turned around, the hospital administrative staff surrounded me. After a brief moment of silence, everyone started talking at the same time. The wave of questions washing in my direction threatened to sweep me off my feet. They all began with "who," "what," "where" or "when." Meanwhile, I was silently asking myself "why" and "how." That is, "Why me?" and "How do I get myself out of this one?" I could not answer even one of their questions!

Fortunately, the "how" came to me. I explained that I had not prepared a presentation because I understood the purpose of today's meeting was to get acquainted and to arrange for my office. I showed them my two manuals, told them that the answers to most of their questions were in these books, and asked if someone could make copies and hand them out. I asked them to sign a list with their name, telephone, and room number, and assured them I would contact each one personally to discuss needs and answer questions. I turned to Dean Blocker and asked him to show me to my new office. As we left the room I performed internal cartwheels of joy and congratulated myself for escaping that room.

While walking down the hall, the Dean explained that the state had only requested one office but he knew I would need more space for my staff (Staff! What staff?), so he arranged for a suite of offices. I was busy digesting the implications of that statement, when we arrived at the door to my new office.

The Dean opened the door and stepped back so I could precede him into the room. The cartwheels of joy collapsed as I stepped around him to peer into a completely empty room. Well, not completely empty—a telephone sat on the floor next to a filthy surgical mat surrounded by empty beer bottles and condom wrappers (someone's love nest, no doubt). When the Dean saw the mess in the room, he apologized and said that he must have opened the wrong door. As we moved down the hall, viewing empty room after empty room, he became increasingly agitated. By the end of the hall, he was furious. He said, "I do not know why your office is not ready, but I will find you a place to be."

Next, we went to the hospital social service office. The director of that office was the person who was supposed to arrange for my office. When the Dean demanded to know why my office was not ready, the director smirked at me and said, "It is not my fault there is no furniture. The Welfare is supposed to provide that." The Dean looked at me for confirmation. I shrugged and said I did not know anything about that, but said I would certainly check into it.

The Dean's next statement wiped the smirk off the director's face. He told him that, until my office was ready, the director was to give me HIS office. After dropping that bombshell, the Dean stalked out of the room. I watched him go, then turned to face a frightened, angry hostile man. For the second time that day I felt like I had been thrown to the wolves and abandoned. This was the person assigned to introduce me to the hospital. Without knowing me, he hated me! OOPS, detour time!

I assured him that I did not want to take his office and that I would be happy with any space he could find for me. The space he found was about the size of a broom closet without a door. There was barely enough room for my desk and chair. My visitor chair and garbage can had to sit in the hall. At least I had a place to put my brief case down and a telephone to call my own. If I wanted to make a private call, I could go sit on the floor in my own office. This is exactly what I did next. I called my boss to find out what in "H#!!" was going on.

When I finally tracked down my manager, he explained that the meeting was a surprise to him too. Since then he learned that the Welfare did not have the budget to set up the office, but the hospital lobbied the State Legislature. My assignment to the hospital was smoke and mirrors to keep them happy until the new budget year when a real office could be funded. He apologized for putting me in a bad situation. However, since I was there I would have to make the best of it and that I should do whatever I could to get an office going with no funds and no staff. Great! So began my new position. To the Welfare I was still a social worker but to the hospital I was the Director of the hospital-based State Department of Public Welfare Office.

This brings me to end of that first day. I realized why the hospital wanted a Welfare office located at the hospital: Medicaid pays hospital and doctor bills. Eligibility for Medicaid was tied to eligibility for welfare. If the welfare application was approved, the Medicaid eligibility date was the date of application. If a patient waited until hospital discharge to apply, the hospital and doctor bills were not covered. The hospital wanted the welfare applications taken before the patient received services so the hospital could cover its expenses.

In fact, Medicare and Medicaid make lots of money for lots of people. It is one way our government subsidizes business in our semi-capitalistic society. People who could not afford medical care could now receive it. These two programs greatly increased the demand for medical care, which subsequently, greatly increased the supply of medical care. This meant more doctors, nurses, pharmacists, physical therapists, etc. This meant more schools, hospitals, clinics, nursing homes, etc. No wonder the hospital administrative staff was excited!

When I got home, I made a list of the positive and negative aspects of my new situation:

On the negative side we had:	On the positive side we had:
No funds	Supplies available from local office
No staff	Enthusiastic hospital staff
Non-functional office	Apparent free hand
Minimal information	
Established enemies	

I knew I needed to learn about Medicare and Medicaid as fast as I could but, in any case, I knew more than the people I would be talking to did. In addition, I could always say, "Good question! I will get back to you on that." The enemies, I would have to turn into friends or neutralize. For the rest, if I was to accomplish anything, I was going to need a lot of help from other people. It was obvious to me that an education program for hospital staff and a paper referral system where essential. I decided to start by visiting the people who attended the first meeting to discuss what they expected from my office and how we might work together.

In six months, I had established a working office by setting up a paper referral system to establish the Medicaid date of application. Upon discharge, the paper work was transferred to the patient's home community.

I could not hire social workers but discovered the limitation did not apply to secretaries. I hired three secretaries to handle paper work, then had social workers detailed from other offices.

The State Department of Public Welfare paid doctors to complete disability reports, so I developed a list of poor residents to complete reports. Since there was no end of starving residents, I had a ready corps of doctors to expedite my reports. I got charts so fast that when a chart was needed in a hurry, hospital staff would call my office rather than the library. Things worked so well the system I established was copied in hospitals all over Texas, and then all over the United States. In fact, things worked so well, eventually I had no work to do and was bored.

You would think that my agency would be pleased with my success, but you would think wrong. About that time I got everything going smoothly, the agency re-organized and I found myself with a new boss. The lady I now worked for had been a nursing home operator at one of the homes I used to visit. She told me that the State Office never expected me to be successful. In fact, they did not want me to succeed because of the costs of the program. Because people came to Sealy from all over the state, there was not a welfare office in

Texas that did not know my name. The local manager was jealous of me, and of the reputation I had gained. She said they wanted to transfer me out of the office and replace me with a plain vanilla worker. Oops! Next time around, maybe I should look for the hidden agenda. Now what was I supposed to do?

52 COCKTAIL WAITRESS

While I was figuring out what to do next, I occupied my time as a bartender/cocktail waitress. This might seem like a strange occupation for a doctor's wife and a social worker, but it all fit in nicely. You remember the summer I worked at Yellowstone as a waitress. Well, at the time, it seemed to me that the cocktail waitresses had a better deal. The load they carried was far lighter than the dinner trays I schlepped around and the more people drank, the bigger the tips seemed to get. One of my social workers had a part-time job as a cocktail waitress and frequently told stories about the bar and its patrons. I told her that it sounded like fun and that if they ever needed someone else, I was interested. As it happened, they called.

I was to work as a cocktail waitress with an experienced bartender at a small private club in a local hotel. At that time, Texas did not allow the sale of liquor by the drink except at private clubs. Therefore, all bars in Texas were either bring-your-own-bottle or private clubs. What made them private was that you had to become a member, which was usually accomplished by filling out a form when you came in and by paying a token fee. It sounds bizarre today, but it was the rule then. The Baptists and the bootleggers kept the law on the books for many years. In fact, what Texas has now is called "local option." This means that in some "dry" areas, you cannot get a drink at all.

Since I had never worked in a bar, the owner suggested I spend an evening at the bar, without pay, to watch what the bartender did. This sounded like a good idea to me. The bartender turned out to be a sleazy-looking, but friendly guy—in fact, too friendly. The last straw was when he offered to show me the counters beneath the bar. When I bent over, he ran his hand up my dress and grabbed my fanny. Having been trained in self-defense, my reaction was to swing first and ask questions later. I scored. He looked upset but did not say anything as I berated him and told him never to try something like that again.

The next evening I arrived at the bar for my first night as a cocktail waitress to find the place dark and unoccupied. I turned on lights, looked around, and then sat down to wait. Opening time came and went with no bartender. I don't know why he didn't show up but I thought it might have something to do with the scene I created the night before. About an hour later, the hotel manager came by to inquire why the bar was closed. I explained the unexplained absence of the bartender. His reply was, "Well, you'd better open. We have a contract." In a panic, I called the owner and his wife told me I should go ahead and open the bar. I said: "I don't know how to mix drinks." She said: "There's a Mr. Boston's Bar Book under the counter but you won't need it. All the patrons drank beer, bourbon, or Scotch." With great apprehension, I moved behind the bar.

My first three customers were an elderly woman and her two sons. Fortunately for me, they opted to sit on the outside patio where they could not see the bar or watch me make the drinks. One man ordered a whiskey sour, one a Black Russian, and the lady ordered a rum drink I had never heard of. I ran back to the bar in a panic—beer, bourbon, or scotch indeed! As it turned out, that was only the first lie the owner's wife told me. Hiding behind the counter, I frantically flipped through the bar book looking for recipes. I knew how a whiskey sour tasted so that one was easy. The Black Russian called for crème de cocoa, which I expected to be brown, but the bottle I found contained white liquor. It tasted like chocolate, so I thought it must be ok. The drink the woman wanted required several types of rum and liquor we did not seem to have. I looked at the woman, considered for a moment, and thought that anyone who ordered a drink that complicated and that sweet probably did not drink much and would not know the difference. I started mixing a combination of things, some in the recipe and some ad-libbed. After I shook it up, I poured a small amount into a glass to taste. Not bad.

When I handed the man the Black Russian (which was white) he said, "Uh, weren't you supposed to make this with brown crème de cacao instead of white?" I thought, "Oh no, they must make crème de cacao in both brown and white!" But I answered, "Yes, but we were out of the brown and they both taste the same." He bought it! When I got back to the bar, I looked for the brown crème de cacao. Sure enough, it comes in both colors and they do taste the same. To this day, I do not really know the difference, if there is any.

Later the woman signaled me to come out to the patio. I thought, "Uh oh, she's going to complain about the drink." Instead, she told me that was the best whatever-it-was she had ever had and gave me a generous tip. I am just grateful she did not order another, because I had no idea what I put in it.

The rest of the evening was uneventful. The patrons did order beer, bourbon or Scotch and I enjoyed visiting with them. Best of all, by the end of the evening I had almost $50.00! This was about $30.00 more a day than my professional job as a social worker paid.

Because of my unorthodox but successful introduction to tending bar, I got the job on a part-time basis, three nights a week. As it turned out, the place had a regular following of people who came almost every night—a Cheers sort of place. Being a bartender is similar to being a social worker with one major difference. As a social worker, I listened to people's problems and gave them encouragement or advice. As a bartender, I listened to people's problems but they became angry if I tried to give them advice. The listening part is the same, but the response is different. At the office I listened, encouraged, or advised. At the bar I listened, encouraged, or commiserated. The people were different also. In my life as a doctor's wife, Medical Dames, the organization for doctor's wives, gave us classes in deportment and how to be an upper class pillar of the community. At the office, I worked with desperately poor people, some with scurvy, malnutrition, and rickets. Mostly blue collar and middle class people came to the bar. The police got into the act also. The Galveston police, who knew I worked at a bar, thought I was a prostitute. The sheriffs, who knew I worked at the courthouse and at a bar, thought I was a narc. It was an interesting time. I enjoyed the activity at the bar, but most of all I enjoyed my shoebox full of money from the bar. Since my babysitting days, it was the first time I actually had disposable funds to spend!

Not too long after I "joined the bar," the owner decided to open a new club. In the 1940s, he had played in a band, and his idea was to open a supper club and bar that featured the big band names of yesterday. He purchased and remodeled an old hole-in-the-wall place that included a bar with a piano, a dance floor, a dining room, and a backroom for high-stake card games. The menu featured choice steak, prime rib, and shrimp. Early afternoon, the down-and-out crowd that had frequented the place before he bought it continued to show up to drink beer and play country music on the juke box. Between five and six, the group that used to come to his prior bar would replace them. The music switched to a mix of country, easy listening, and rock. Between eight and nine the dinner crowd of attorneys and doctors took their place in the dining room, and the high rollers filtered in to the backroom to play cards. The juke box turned off at nine and the entertainment began.

On weeknights, the entertainment was usually a piano player, with a sing-along book. On the weekends, the featured attraction turned to a low-dollar version of Las Vegas. Usually there was a band, sometimes with a singer, dancer, or comedian. Most of the acts were once famous, now down on their luck, but still going. Several of them were names I remember from listening to the radio late at night while babysitting. The most memorable, for me, was Sally Rand. Most of you are probable too young to have heard of Sally Rand, the first fan dancer. At the bar, she danced totally nude to "Clair de Lune" while she maneuvered two large, white, feathered fans. It was a great show! As she danced, she moved the fans in such a way that, nothing was exposed, unless you were standing behind her, as I was at the bar. Then you got a view of the full Monty.

When I first saw her, I thought it was sad that a woman of her age was still performing. She told me she was 67, but from her stories, I think she was closer to 80. I asked her how she got started. She told me that, when she was young, she was offered a job as a stripper. She said she was desperate for a job, but knew that she could not expose herself in front of an audience. Then she had the idea of using the fans. When I saw her dance and her reaction to applause, I realized it was a blessing she could still dance at her age. The dance was who she was. I would like to think that when I am in my '80s I might still be able to flip a fan or two.

I included the last paragraphs for two reasons: When the club expanded, so did my income. I made almost twice as much. If you plan to work in a club, find a busy one with a crowd you enjoy. The second reason was to include Sally Rand. If you really need to earn some money, look what she did with nothing but her birthday suit and a few feathers.

53 ARTIST MODEL

This is one of those fun jobs that require no work – unless you are like me and find it difficult to sit and do nothing. One of the bar patrons was a popular local painter. His forte was large landscape/seascape scenes that looked great over the mantel. The state tourist bureau featured him in a series of ads to portray the beauty of the state.

One night at the club, he asked if I would model for him. In my naiveté, I said yes. I was thrilled. I was familiar with his work and thought of him rather like Norman Rockwell–all-American clean.

Less well known was the fact that he painted nude portraits for select clients. When he asked me to model, it never even occurred to me that he might expect me to model nude or that he might paint me as a nude! Even when he told me I could bring my swimsuit, I thought it was because his studio was on the beach and he was inviting me to swim afterwards.

Understanding finally dawned when I arrived at his studio and he asked me to undress. Boy, was I embarrassed! Fortunately, when he understood my misunderstanding, he laughed. The reason he wanted to paint me was that I had hair long enough to sit on.

We worked out a compromise: I would wear my swimsuit; he would paint a nude with my hair, but with a different face and complexion. No one was to know it was me.

In the dressing room, when I put on my custom-made, itsy, bitsy, tiny weeny bikini I realized that I had gained a little weight since last I wore it and had a small pot where my flat stomach should be. I hoped he wouldn't notice it. Much to my chagrin, the stomach was the first thing he noticed. He said, "Oh, that's really great! It'll make the picture more believable."

When the artist finished, the woman in the painting looked like a South Sea beauty with brown skin and long, silky, black hair—not me at all. I asked him who he painted the picture for, but he wouldn't tell me and I never saw it again.

Our compromise took all the fun and most of the glamour out of being an artist's model but was certainly safer for my standing in the community as a social worker and a doctor's wife. And after all, I did earn $30. Not bad, considering minimum wage in 1969 was $1.60 an hour.

54 QUALITY CONTROL & # 55 QUALITY ASSURANCE

A friend of mine was promoted to the State Welfare Office in Austin as the Director of Quality Control. In 1970, he called to ask, "Would you like to come work for me as a quality control reviewer?" I said, "Yes!" The job was a bird's nest on the ground. Quality Control was managed out of Austin, but, for the most part, reviewers worked at homes. Assignments were mailed to reviewers, who scheduled their own work and traveled to offices across the state. The work consisted of reviewing a random sample of cases selected by the Federal Government to determine if staff had followed policy/procedures and if the client was eligible for the benefits received.

My territory was the southern part of Texas from Louisiana to New Mexico and from Austin to the Mexican border. As long as work was turned in on time, no one questioned where I was or what I did. I loved the job because I really enjoyed travel and eating at new places. We also had meetings around the state and sometimes worked as a group on fraud investigations with the FBI.

When we were on the road together, my co-workers were a tall lanky West Texas cowboy, a gay guy from Houston, and a short Mexican from the valley. The boys treated me like one of the guys. The cowboy was partial to honky-tonks. The Mexican took us places that would not be safe for a gringo alone and the gay guy took us to bars where I was safe, but I'm not so sure about the guys. Although so totally different, we really got along well. We all liked to eat and we all liked to dance. When I think back to those days, it seems we waltzed across Texas.

Not too long after I joined the group, the federal government changed the sample period and for a while we had no work to do. I was assigned temporarily to the Quality Assurance Review Team. This was another great job. The Quality Assurance team traveled to a location as a group. The manager went to the local office and returned with boxes of case folders. These were assigned to us for desk review to determine if all the required paper work was in the folder and complete. My first trip was to Corpus Christi, Texas, where we rented a bungalow on the beach. By the end of the first day, I finished reviewing all the cases assigned to me and took them back to the manager. I thought he would be pleased with my work and was not prepared for his reaction. He was extremely upset. He told me I had finished all the work for a week and that, if I did not slow down, I was going to ruin a good thing for all of them.

He returned the folders to me and told me to turn in a few folders each day. When I asked him what I was supposed to do for the rest of the week he said, "I don't care. Why don't you go fishing?" Hey, OK by me! A paid vacation is the best kind! Needless to say, I was sorry when the temporary assignment ended.

While working for Quality Control, I went back to school to finish my B.A. When I left college, I needed only 15 hours to graduate. I planned to finish someday, but kept putting it off because I would need 30 hours at another school to graduate. On day, a friend asked why I had not returned to school. My excuses was that I would be so much older than the other students and it would take two years of night school to finish. She said, "How old will you be in two years?" I said, "30." She said, "Well, in two years, you can be 30 with a degree or you can be 30 without one." I thought, "You know, she is right!" I registered that afternoon.

One of the interesting things I did in college was a two-year research project to study the value of welfare entitlement. I mention this here, because it is a source for money—not a route to riches or even a way I have personally tried, but something to check into in the right (or wrong) circumstances.

My interest in the subject came from what I saw on my job. As a social worker in the '60s, I visited shotgun shacks and saw people in deplorable conditions with scurvy, malnutrition, and rickets. As a quality control reviewer in the '70s, I interviewed a random sample of welfare recipients, most of whom lived in three-bedroom brick houses with a Pontiac in the driveway. The amount of the welfare check in

Texas had not changed during that period. I obtained permission to use the random sample data and to ask some additional questions. What I learned was that the Great Society Programs, implemented during the Kennedy and Johnson eras, had changed the face of poverty in America. In the early '60s, the check was the only welfare benefit. By the '70s, eligibility for welfare brought a Pandora's box of additional entitlement, such as food stamps, housing supplements, utility assistance, medical benefits, day care supplements, assistance in obtaining child support, Pell grants for college, and referrals for Social Security, VA benefits and unemployment. Federal, state and county agencies other than welfare administer most of these programs. Therefore, none of the public records pulled the whole picture together.

What I found was that legitimately eligible welfare recipients, living in urban areas with access to other benefit programs, had household income equivalent to three times the poverty level. In rural areas, recipients without access to the other programs had income three times below poverty level. The data indicated that our system for determining eligibility for welfare and amount of entitlement does not work. The programs presume steady, monthly income, where most welfare clients' monthly income varies greatly. I got an 'A' in the course.

Now it seems as though Congress is determined to roll us back to the days of scurvy and malnutrition. However, if you are down on your luck, do not forget to check into what might be available from the state, county or federal government to tide you over until you figure out something better.

56 ARTIST

In 1972 when I divorced my husband. The attorney who handled my divorce had numerous oil paintings around his office. When I complemented the pictures, he said, "I painted most of them." He told me he was a member of a group that rented a studio and painted with a local artist every week. That sounded like fun to me. I had never tried painting with oils but it was on my list of things to try. He told me the group was short one member. If I agreed to pay a share of the rent, I could join.

The studio was on the second floor of an old mansion in Galveston with an ocean view. It had 16-foot ceilings and balconies. An art gallery with a wraparound Victorian porch occupied the first floor. The group met one night a week but we could use the space any time we wanted. For my part, it was love at first sight. I loved the building, I loved the people, and I loved to paint. All of the people in the group painted with palette knives and were happy to share their techniques. To me, painting with a palette knife is like finger painting. It is quick and easy. As the colors mix, you automatically build in depth, shadow, and light.

Although I did not know it at the time, I do have a talent for painting. I assumed I could not paint because I did not think I could draw. However, the issue turned out to be seeing, not drawing. I was born legally blind but did not get glasses until I was seven. What I saw before I got glasses was not form, but color. Therefore, I could do things with paint that I never dreamed I could. The studio immediately became my home away from home.

After three weeks, my first painting was dry enough to take home. As I descended the front stairs of the studio, a woman stopped me and asked to see my picture. She praised it. I was so proud because I had done something I did not think I could. When I told her I painted the picture, she said, "Will you sell it to me?" After I got over the shock, I said yes. She gave me the price I asked, took my painting, and left me standing on the steps in a daze. I was an ARTIST! Someone actually paid money for something I did! Later, I realized that the painting was worth much more to me in emotional value than the money I received, but the validation was appreciated.

Most of the people in the group considered themselves "Sunday artists," people who painted for pleasure but occasionally sold some work at weekend art shows or in consignment galleries. Although I sold my first effort, I did not have the confidence to try a show or gallery. Three things changed my opinion. After I filled my walls and the walls of my family and friends, I did not have anywhere to put the canvases I produced in quantity. Next, though not prohibitive, the supplies do cost money. The turning point came when I was visiting one of the local consignment galleries and saw a woman pay a small fortune for what I thought was one of the ugliest pictures I had ever seen. I went out that afternoon and made arrangements to buy frames wholesale. By the end of the week, my backlog of paintings was on display in the gallery.

In my optimism, I expected immediate sales. This did not happen, but by the end of the month, my paintings were all sold. One sold to a 12-year-old boy who brought in his piggy bank and paid in coin. The story really touched me. If I had been there when it happened, I would have given it to him. When I think about my early search for a product to sell, it still seemed somewhat unreal that people would pay for something I painted.

One of My Oil Paintings

Before long, I had my paintings in three galleries and received requests for custom paintings. The sales income now exceeded the cost, so I showed a real profit. I still had my day job, though. But I was on my way to becoming a professional artist.

57 QUALITY CONTROL SUPERVISOR

In 1972, four months after I got my degree, I was promoted to management as a Quality Control Supervisor and transferred back to Houston. My job was to supervise staff, assign work, review work, analyze the findings, and recommend corrective actions and ways to improve the process. The job also involved conducting standards training classes for employees.

Initially, I was concerned about teaching. (Remember my previous experience!) However, none of my fears came to be. I may have bored some people to death, but at least I did not get any dumb stares. I found I really enjoyed the classes.

Since I had managed staff before, that part of the job did not present any more challenges than working with people normally does. However, I will mention one incident that may help someone else.

I had a secretary who was a very sweet person and seemed to be intelligent. She did most assignments well and on time. However, her one failing was that she could not file. I established what I thought was a decent filing system and gave her a detailed index. When I learned that things were not filed where they should be, I assumed she did not understand the system. I spent several sessions explaining the system and expanding the definitions on the index. When this did not produce results, I annotated correspondence and reports with the name of the file where they were to be placed. When this did not work, in exasperation, I said, "What's the matter? Can't you see?" Later I felt bad about my remark and apologized to her.

About two weeks later, she came into my office to say thank you. She said she thought about what I said, and went to an eye doctor to have her eyes checked. It turned out she was legally blind. She was in her twenties, had never had her eyes checked, and thought everyone saw a blurry world. How would you know if no one ever told you? If you spend a lot of time bumping into walls, you might want to get your eyes checked.

58 ART TEACHER

Something I missed when I moved to Houston was my studio group. I was still painting but missed the companionship of the group and the opportunity to learn new techniques. To fill the gap, I signed up for art classes and seminars. I moved from palette knife to brush or did combination paintings.

The first portrait I painted was of a co-worker's father, based on a Depression-era photograph. When I saw it I knew I wanted to paint it. It was mine to keep, but so obviously belonged to his family that I gave it to him.

One of my art instructors had been a grade school teacher and gave very clear directions. I taped a seminar she gave. Several people in the class offered to pay me to transcribe the notes. When I gave them copies they all had trouble following the written word and asked if I would teach a class using the notes. I questioned whether I knew enough to teach painting but decided "You teach best that which you need to learn." Since I enjoyed the company and painting so much, I think I got more out of the classes than I gave—plus, I was paid. This was my first, but not my last teaching job.

59 ADMINISTRATOR

After six months as a manager, in 1973 I was promoted to Assistant Director of the Medicaid Program and moved to Austin, Texas. I was 31 years old. Not long after I moved to the State Office, I discovered I was seventh highest in the bureaucratic hierarchy and was the token female administrator. There were people who commented about how quickly I had been promoted. (Ten years with the agency is quick?)

One morning the first week on the job, my boss called me about 7:00 a.m. and said, "You need to pack a bag. I'm sending you to Washington, D.C. to negotiate changes in the Medicaid contract between Texas and the federal government." After I picked myself up off the floor, I asked him to repeat what he just said. Once I understood he was not kidding, I said, "Are you sure I can handle this?" He said, "Yes, I'll answer all your questions when you get here, but you'd better hurry. Your plane leaves at 11:30 this morning." With great apprehension I started throwing things into a suitcase.

Although states were responsible for Medicaid program administration, most of the costs were paid by the federal government. I later learned that funding was a tool used by the federal government to get the states to do what the Feds wanted done and to maintain control. Once programs were established the federal match would decrease however, the Feds would still try to maintain control. The process lent itself to some interesting game-playing behavior.

In Texas, the Medicaid budget was two billion dollars a year so this was no small game. The state's role was to maximize federal funding while minimizing federal control. The federal role was the reverse. No one wanted the programs to end because our own jobs and salaries were tied up in the game. The whole process reminded me of a cross between a poker game and a kiddy argument.

A year later, the Director of Medicaid quit and I was promoted to his job. You might think this would make me sixth highest in the bureaucracy, but it did not. In the preceding year the bureaucracy had added enough upper level positions that, though I got a grade and salary increase, I was 27th highest. Eligibility determination for Medicaid and cash assistance for aged, blind and disabled people was transferred to the federal government. However, administration of Medicaid remained the responsibility of the state. This meant that I became the administrator of a computer exchange.

In the early days of the transfer of responsibility, a computer error resulted in the pre-mature demise (at least in the computer) of a number of Medicaid recipients who were, in fact, not dead. Since the programmers for the system did not believe in resurrection of the dead, there was no way to re-instate the erroneously diseased. While we tried to figure out how to resurrect the dead and stop the computer from killing more people, the "living dead" were storming the capital demanding benefits and our heads. Because I successfully resolved this problem, I was labeled a "computer expert" when most people were totally unaware that computers were about to overrun our world.

60 INCOME TAX

This may seem like a strange way to make money but I promise it is one of the most powerful tools you can use to increase your wealth. If you want more money at your disposal, you can either increase your income or decrease your expenses. Decreasing taxes so you can keep more of the money you make is one of the best ways to decrease expenses.

In 1973 when I was a supervisor in Houston, Texas my gross salary was $675 a month. The Assistant Director position paid $1,675 a month. When I got my first pay check I was expecting a fortune. Can you imagine my disappointment when my take home pay was all of $25 a month more than I made as a manager? How could that be!

The answer turned out to be federal income tax. At that time the maximum income tax rate was 70%. My ex-husband and I had a tax attorney who advised us on tax matters and filed our returns. Since we owned a home and both of us were in school, we had enough deductions that we paid no taxes. After my divorce in 1972, I had no tax deductions. To add insult to injury, when tax time rolled around I owed an additional $5,000. I decided it was time to learn about tax deductions.

What I found was that our tax system is not only about collecting money to run the government; it is an income redistribution system. Congress uses tax deductions and credits to encourage behavior members (or their large contributors) want. I see the tax system as being like the rules of Monopoly because what is taxed and what is deductible can have a major impact on your bottom line.

If you structure your financial affairs to take advantage of the tax laws, the Government lets you keep more of your own money and do your own distribution. If you don't, they take your money and distribute it for you. Once I understood this principle, I studied tax law and restructured my activities to take advantage of legitimate tax deductions. Many start-up business fail because they don't understand these principles. They count money taken in as profit without taking business expenses and taxes into consideration. I know this happens because I've done so myself.

Many tax deductions are related to owning your own business. I was already selling my paintings so the first thing I did was to form a company called Enterprising Artist. This turned the expense of buying paint supplies into a tax deduction. It also allowed me to get a sales tax permit which gave me access to tax-free goods and to wholesale markets such as the Dallas Trade Mart, a Pandora's Box of goodies.

Over time I've used Enterprising Artist as the umbrella for most of my money-making activities. At different times in my life I've used my company to deduct such things as a home office, travel expenses, supplies and inventory. (As a side note my company logo was a little armadillo with a parachute and skies. Years later I recognized the resemblance to the fool card in the Taro deck.)

The next thing I did was to buy a house. The deduction for mortgage interest is one way our government supports home ownership and is the largest tax deductions most people have.

Over the next few years at tax time, I would sort expenses as tax-deductible and non-deductible. Then I would review the non-deductible expenses to see if there was any way I could legitimately make them tax-deductible. For example, at that time interest on a car payment and on credit cards was deductible. I bought a car and applied for credit cards.

Today income tax rates are lower with fewer deductions and tax credits have been added. However, tax law still can have a major impact on your bottom line.

61 STAINED GLASS ARTIST

In addition to being "Ms. Welfare," I spent my spare time on my hobbies. For years, I wanted to learn how to work with stained glass. In Houston, I took a class and made one window. If I wanted to become proficient, I knew I would need to make many more. Since the materials were so expensive I told my friends that I planned to make stained glass sun catchers and sell them at arts and craft shows. Upon moving to Austin, I turned into a couch potato and became proficient at procrastinating.

Stained Glass Window I Made

One day, my best friend called my bluff. She told me that I had better get busy because she signed me up for a Christmas craft show. To prove she was not bluffing, she handed me the receipt. I had four months to create some inventory.

By show time, I had a collection of sun catchers complete with macramé hangers, plus my oil paintings. Most of the paintings were what I considered rejects. However, my friend insisted that I frame them and take them to the show; the first painting to sell was one she pulled out of the garbage.

The day of the show, I looked at my stuff, then looked at everyone else's stuff, and decided mine would never sell. In a moment of panic, I thought about what I was going to do with all the leftovers. I signed up for a second show. By the end of the day, everything was sold. Now, I had another problem, inventory for the next show. I arranged to take off from work and went into full-time production. I sold out at the second show as well. This of course led to more stained glass creations and more shows. At one point, I could have quit my day job and gone into stained glass full time. In fact, one of the roads I investigated but did not follow was to open a stained glass shop in the old town in Geneva, Switzerland. I looked into visas and locations but chickened out before I became an expatriate.

By now, you might think that I was a fantastic artist. You would be wrong—I was good at marketing. I was doing so well at the shows that I convinced the owner of the store where I bought my stained glass supplies that she should sell at an arts and craft show. Unlike me, she is a "real" artist. In fact, she now designs for Corning Glass Works.

I felt like eating my encouragement when I discovered she had a booth close to mine at the next show. Her stuff was wonderful and in the same price range as mine. I felt sick. I was sure I would sell nothing. However, by the end of the show, I sold out and she still had most of her inventory. It boggled my mind. I set out to find out why my stuff sold while her superior stuff (at the same price) did not sell. That is when I learned the value of marketing.

My First Craft Show Booth

To summarize, my booth layout made it comfortable for people to step in and browse. Her booth was closed in. Most of the buyers were middle class housewife types who wanted to feel good about themselves and what they bought. I dressed for, visited with, and related to the crowd. She and her boyfriend were hippies in dress and manners. They spent most of the show scowling at the customers. The moral here is that the better mousetrap does not always sell; the marketed mousetrap is usually the one the customer takes home.

62 PROMOTER

While selling at craft shows, I thought it was awfully nice of the promoters to go to all that trouble just so artists could have a place to sell their stuff. Boy, was I dumb. It finally dawned on me what the promoters got for their effort. They got the gate.

Arts and craft shows are generally set up where the artists pay booth fees for the space they occupy and patrons pay a fee at the door. The promoters use the artists' money to pay upfront costs, like space rental and advertising, and then they get the admission money. At the show where I learned that promoters were not art patrons but capitalists, I made $2,000 as an artist; the promoters made $27,000.

I found a house I wanted to buy and needed money. I decided to organize an arts and craft show and asked two friends to go in with me. We each put up $300.00. With this money, we paid a deposit to rent the city auditorium and paid for ads for artist participation.

Because it was our first show, ads to attract artist cost more than expected. In fact, signing up artists was the hardest part of organizing the show. Without them, we had no show and no money to pay expenses. (The need for artists explains why we passed around what turned out to be an obscene telephone call.)

One night a man called to say he was interested in renting space at our show but was not sure if we would accept his type of art. Of course, I asked, "What type would that be?" "Nudes," he replied, as he graphically described his work. I told him I personally had no objection, but perhaps he should talk to my partners. I gave him their numbers. After talking to him, my most suspicious partner checked with the city auditorium to determine if nude art was allowed. The auditorium people told her that there was no prohibition, but said we might want to be careful. If anyone was offended, the show's promoters could be arrested for selling pornography! In fact, one promoter used this tactic to get a rival show closed. We added liability insurance to the list of things to buy and decided to tell the caller no.

At our next meeting, we discussed the artist who had asked about nudes. He had called us all but had not called back to sign up for the show. One partner said, "Do you suppose he could be an obscene caller?" We compared notes. Based on his graphic descriptions we concluded he was. How embarrassing! First, not to recognize an obscene telephone call, and next to pass the caller on to friends!

Besides learning to recognize obscene telephone calls, I learned a lot from this show. I organized and conducted the ad campaign. I did radio, television, newspaper, and magazine ads. From a non-profit silent auction, I acquired two billboards and several street banners. For this show, we did everything I wanted in a show. We provided setup, takedown assistance, coffee, and donuts, change, Visa and MasterCard charge services, and play care for the kids. The show was a rousing success. After taxes, and dividing with my partners, I still earned enough for the down payment to buy the house.

Speaking of taxes, the show was a real revelation for me. Even though it was only a one- day show, we had to file a partnership business return, pay workman's compensation, income and Social Security taxes for our one-day employees, as well as income tax and self-employment Social Security tax for ourselves. Each of us added 10 pages to our tax returns and helped a CPA pay his mortgage.

After the show, artists wrote and called to ask when we planned to do another show. Because I was stupid, the answer was "never." Both my partners wanted to do another show with me but had a falling out and did not want to do another show with each other. I still had my day job; I got what I wanted out of this show; and I did not want to lose either collaborators as a friend. Oh well, one of those forks in the road! If I had been thinking of a long-term business opportunity rather than a short-term way to reach a goal, I would have continued the shows and left my day job far behind.

63 GARAGE SALES

I fell in love with the house the first time I saw it. As you no doubt know, love is blind. That's how I failed to notice small things like the fact that the kitchen had no electrical outlets (there was a gas refrigerator complete with instructions on how to make ice cubes) and a gaping hole in the bathroom that allowed the sun to shine on the porcelain throne. For the next couple of years, I spent my spare time remodeling and furnishing the house I bought.

My first morning in the house, I was ensconced on the commode reading the paper when my "library time" was rudely interrupted by what I thought was a rat falling on my paper from the hole in the ceiling. I screamed and stood up. The rat fell to the floor and assumed a rigor mortis stance. I had just noticed how peculiar the rat looked when he opened one eye, looked at me, then jumped up and ran away. I ran to the telephone and called an exterminator.

After looking around, the exterminator informed me that the rat was a baby opossum; that I was "blessed" with a whole nest of them and that they were a protected species and could not be killed. He told me I would have to put out live traps or carry a broom around with me. He said, "Opossums play dead." He explained that if I carried a broom, I could hit them when I saw them and they would play dead. Then I could pick them up, put them in a box, and take them to the country for release. He also told me to put wire over any openings to the house so no more could get in. However, he advised I wait until I caught all the ones living in my house as the smell of dead opossum in the walls left something to be desired.

After he left, my dog, my cat, my broom, and I went to the yard to work. You know that feeling when you think someone is watching you? When I looked around I saw no one. However, when I looked up, I saw 32 beady eyes staring at me from the gutter. There were 16 baby opossums in all. It took a month for me to round them all up and take them to the country. In the meantime, I called the bank and learned that I could not get a remodel loan for six months. Since six months is a long time to live with no electricity in your kitchen, a hole in your bathroom, and the fear of falling opossums, I needed to find a way to raise some quick money.

The garage provided the opportunity I was looking for. I paid the former owner $10.00 for the contents of the double car garage. At first glance it all looked like trash. However, buried under the trash was every collectable you ever dreamed of finding. I found crystal, china and silver pieces and sets; collectable kitchen ware and utensils, pottery plates, bowls, mugs and flower pots; tin, enamel and copper pots and pans; souvenirs from the first world's fair; political buttons and US postage stamps, dolls, jewelry and tools as well as furniture. One of the real treasures was a pecan dresser-wash stand combination with a full length mirror and a marble top that dated to the early nineteenth century that I still have today. If I had properly marketed the contents of the garage, I probably could have paid the $24,000 price for the house with money left over. Instead, I invited all my friends over to take anything they wanted. After we all took what we wanted, there was still a lot of stuff.

I decided to have a garage sale to clear the place out and invited the same friends to join me with anything they wanted to sell. We ended up with furniture and stuff lined down the driveway and a weekend party. By Sunday, I was four thousand dollars richer and had more stuff left in the garage than when I started. None of my friends took their things that didn't sell home.

This was the start of my garage sale business. I gave up my goal of getting my car in the garage and started collecting stuff for the next garage sale. I enjoyed going to garage sales, so now I not only bought stuff I wanted for myself I bought stuff that was underpriced for re-sale. I ran two sales a year out of the garage.

My garage became the temporary storage and dumping ground for all the stuff my friends wanted to get rid of or wanted to sell. I never knew when I came home what would be there. One day the garage was filled with business envelops. It took me two weeks to find the owner. One of my friends bid on a damaged shipment from an insurance company but did not want the envelopes when they were delivered. I made $1,500 selling manila envelopes at three cents apiece.

I used to joke that my garage had everything in it except the kitchen sink. Then, one day I found a turquoise colored kitchen sink, along with a tub and commode, had been added to the pile by one of my friends. I also discovered that a lot of the stuff I sold ended up at the consignment stores for re-sale. If I'd been really smart I would have taken the stuff there in the first place!

64 FURNITURE REFINISHING

Furnishing my house from garage sales automatically lead to the acquisition of a lot of old furniture in need of some help. Today, they tell us not to refinish antiques because it reduces the value. Then the focus was not on value as much as on function and appearance. I wanted stuff that looked nice and people charged more for furniture that was refinished. Professional refinishing offset the savings from buying the piece at a garage sale or auction. By now, you know my solution. I learned how to refinish furniture. But first I had to learn what was worth refinishing

One day a friend called in tears to complain about the awful furniture her husband bought for their bedroom. She was so upset I offered to go to her house to see the furniture. I thought it really couldn't be that bad, but it was. The bedroom set was painted puke yellow and really did look awful.

Several weeks later I stopped by to visit my friend. When she showed me her bedroom I was totally amazed. Instead of puke yellow the furniture was a beautiful golden oak with an inlayed design. I could not believe it was the same furniture and congratulated her on talking her husband out of the other stuff. She said, "It is the same furniture. My husband refinished it."

I could not wait to ask him how he knew what was under the awful paint. He explained that he didn't know about the inlay but that he did know the style of the furniture and that it was oak. When I asked him how he knew he gave me a funny look and said, "I learned about antiques and wood." He suggested I visit lumber stores to learn about the different woods and stains and go to antique stores and junk shops to learn about furniture and hardware. That is exactly what I did along with reading about antiques and collectables and learning how to refinish furniture.

Furniture refinishing is messy and can be dangerous work. First, I only refinished things for my own home. Overtime, I replaced some refinished pieces with new refinished pieces and relegated the old pieces to the garage to be sold at the next sale. These pieces always sold first and for far more than I paid for them. The more furniture I refinished, the more sophisticated my refinishing set up and skills became. Eventually, I refinished furniture for resale in my twice-yearly garage sale and occasionally took pieces to consignment stores. This can be a very profitable side line if you like to work with wood and have the storage space. Today most of my house is furnished with pieces I bought at junk stores, auctions and garage sales and refinished.

65 SAVERR PROJECT MANAGER

(Texas; Health and Human Services)

Because of my "expertise" with computers, in 1975 the Commissioner asked me to lead a computer system design effort called SAVERR, System for Application, Verification, Eligibility, Referrals, and Reporting. Originally assigned to the information systems area, the project to design a generic welfare system for the State of Texas was behind schedule and over budget.

To design the system, I formed a task group of the "kings and queens of the agency's mountains" (Food Stamps, Aid to Families with Dependent Children, Medicaid, Social Services and Information Technology.). We spent the next five years trying to kill each other in a long, skinny room with no windows. However, we succeeded in creating a system that survived from the seventies until the Y2K bug finally forced a redesign in 2000. At the time, the only larger set of computer code was the Apollo programming written to put man on the moon.

Actually, the first attempt succeeded in three years, but the system was programmed using IBM-patented software. While we were developing the system, the state legislature forced a competitive bid for computer equipment and acquired Unisys hardware. We spent the last two years converting everything to run on the Unisys platform.

When we finished the system design, I went to work with our Medicaid contractor on the interface between their system and our new system. When I started working with the interface, out of a million records, there were a quarter million with mismatched data. By the time I finished, the error rate was .004 % and costs were down by thirty million dollars. (I wish I worked on a percentage of savings but I did not.)

The only reason there was any error rate at all was a disagreement about whether 1900 was a leap year. If you are like me, you probable assumed that leap year has always been with us, but this turned out not to be the case. There are many different calendars in the world, each with its own way of adjusting calendar dates to match the earth's rotation around the sun. Today the internationally accepted civil calendar is the Gregorian calendar. This was first introduced in 1582 and defines leap year as we now know it. However until the late nineteenth century there was no universally accepted standard. With the advent of the railroad, such things as date and time took on more importance in daily life.

In 1901 some bureaucrats finally decided to address the problem by establishing The National Institutes of Standards and Technology (NIST.) NIST adopted the Gregorian calendar as the US standard. However, implementation lagged somewhat across the country and the world. This led to variable interpretations of leap year and problems with interpreting a few birth dates between systems. Texas uses the NIST standards. The contractor's code was based on a different date researched by a hotshot programmer. The programmer's authority was such that the contractor refused to alter the code. When I requested the change and stated my reason, the response was, "Who do you expect us to believe, you or our programmer?" Thus the .004% error rate.

There is a lesson or two here. First, we tend to take for granted "what is." The truth is most things like our assumptions about time and date are just that, assumptions. Someone sometime decided to do something a particular way and we assume that is the way it inevitably is. However, it does not have to be that way. Things change and can be changed.

Frequently, change is where the money is. You know the old saw about building a better mousetrap. Another thing, since I was paying the bill, I assumed the contractor should do things my way. The results affirmed that "to assume makes an ass of u and me." Just because you pay the bill does not guarantee you get it your way.

66 PALMIST

I do not know if you have ever looked into non-credit classes at your local college, but if you haven't, now is the time to do so. Most colleges and universities offer a wide range of classes to fit the needs and interests of almost everyone. The University of Texas at Austin had a fine program. I had taken several art and music classes I enjoyed and decided to try pottery. Unfortunately, the pottery classes were full. However, nestled in the "Ps" in the catalogue, I found "Introduction to Palmistry."

When I was in junior high, a friend's mother read palms. I thought that might be interesting. My motive for taking the class was that it would be a great way to meet and visit with guys while we sat holding hands.

In the class, I learned that the purpose of palmistry is not fortune telling, but personal growth. There are "classical" interpretations for the size, shape, lines, mounds, and marks on the hands. The theory is that your genetic makeup and birth family tend to make you react and respond in certain ways. Of your two hands, one (your genetic hand) shows what was intended and the other hand shows what you are making of your life. For example, if you are right-handed, your left hand is your genetic hand and your right hand shows what you are making of your life.

A trained palmist looks at things like your head line, heart line and life line on both hands, and then compares them to each other and to the classical interpretations for these lines. Some palmists also claim to be psychic. I wasn't sure about that, but I learned that it helps to be attentive, intuitive, and able to spin a good story.

As a predominately left-brained individual, I decided to leave the psychic out of my studies and concentrate on memorizing the meanings. This led to some clumsy early readings. For example, flex your fingers and thumb backwards. If there is a lot of give, you are supposed to be flexible and adaptive in your approach to life. If there is little give, you are supposed to be rigid and set in your ways.

The first time I tried this on a co-worker, the woman was stiff as a board. I was surprised because I knew her to be extremely easygoing and adaptable. Nevertheless, I gave her the "text book" interpretation. Her response: "No, dear, that just means I have arthritis." Well, so much for the left-brained approach.

When I finished the first course, the teacher told me I had promise, so I signed up for the advanced course. I told all my friends and co-workers I was taking palmistry, and since I did not charge anything, I got plenty of practice reading palms.

One New Year's Eve at a friend's party, I was approached by a woman who read Tarot cards. She suggested that we form a team and get an agent to book us for parties. Being "three sheets to the wind" (it was New Year's Eve after all) I said yes, never expecting anything to come of it.

Within a week, we had an agent and Madam Viviana was born. For the next couple of years, I was paid to dress as a gypsy, go to parties, and read palms. I eventually moved on to other things. However, to this day, my partner makes her living through a 1-900 Dial-a-Psychic network. If I ever need money badly, I can hang a palm sign out the window and resume business.

67 COMMUNITY SCHOOL TEACHER

While I was taking the palmistry course at the University of Texas, the local school system decided to offer continuing education classes. The elementary school two blocks from my house contacted me to see if I would like to teach painting, stained glass, or palmistry. The pay was not tremendous, but it was an enjoyable way to meet people and make a little money on the side.

Over several semesters, I managed to teach all three subjects as well as take several classes myself. A side benefit to teaching was to increase the patrons for my own art. I sold quite a few stained glass sun catchers and some paintings; I also read a few palms. Between the art galleries, the shows and the palmistry gigs, I made enough money that I considered quitting my day job—but not yet.

68 CARNIVAL GAMES

It was carnival games that eventually convinced me to leave my day job for greener (?) pastures. Most towns have some annual festival to commemorate something or to raise money for something. As a citywide block party, Austin Texas has Aqua Fest. "Aqua" means water in Spanish. This might seem a strange name for a festival in a landlocked city in dry Texas, but the Colorado River runs through the town. One of the features of Aqua Fest is a boat parade.

The Chamber of Commerce sponsors Aqua Fest to bring people and business into downtown Austin and to raise money to support various non-profit activities, not the least of which is putting on Aqua Fest. Volunteers and vendors do all the work and everyone spends ten summer evenings hanging out at the river listening to music, drinking and eating. Not a bad life if you can get it.

I volunteered to work at Aqua Fest for several years. During that time, it went from a friend- and family-oriented event to a commercial entertainment event featuring nationally known singers and bands. The adults wanted to listen to the music, dance, and drink, but there was no place to stash the kids. We decided to establish Little Fest, an area to feature kids' games and activities.

I was assigned to find non-profit groups willing to set up game booths in Little Fest. I found willing groups, but no one knew what to do. Since figuring out what to do is one of my specialties, I started to research carnival games. What I found was a whole world of fairs and festivals along with national associations, newsletters, and magazines.

This search eventually gave me an understanding of our distribution system, took me into the world of the Mexican Mafia and led to imports, but I am getting ahead of my story. I helped groups such as the Boy Scouts, the Battered Women's Center and the March of Dimes decide what to do and to locate necessary materials and supplies, such as carnival prizes. In addition to the large prizes, state law required consolation prizes for all carnival-type games. I put a lot of effort into locating good games and affordable prizes from stuffed toys to plastic flags and piggy banks.

As the starting date approached, we still had empty booths. The commander for Little Fest suggested that I take the remaining five booths and run them for profit. I convinced a number of friends to help and choose a color/number wheel (similar to a roulette wheel where you bet on a color, a number or both), cork guns, darts, penny pitch and a water balloon toss.

Each game presented its own set of problems. For example, cork guns are a popular attraction, but choosing something to shoot turned out to be a problem. My first attempt was a set of cute animal cutouts. These turned out to be too cute to shoot and too heavy to knock over with a cork gun, plus I don't like the idea of killing anything. We finally settled on some small plastic piggybanks I bought for consolation prizes. If you put a penny in the slot, the bank was heavy enough not to blow off the shelf but hard enough to hit that you would not give the store away.

Color/number wheels were expensive to buy so I decided to make my own. To start, I cut two lopsided circles out of plywood and divided each into twelve sections painted a different color. Next a friend and I spent most of a day trying to drill center holes in the circles. Through persistence and brute force, we finally got one hole drilled; then a male friend stopped by and pointed out that the drill was set to reverse. Setting the drill properly speeded up the process considerably. Unfortunately, the combination of the lopsided circles with off-center holes resulted in a color/number wheel that always stopped in the same place. Not a winner for the owner of such a wheel! The same male friend helped us round the circle and suggested a ball bearing center.

Efforts to correct the wobble and figure out what to use as a pointer and stops proved as much of a challenge as learning how to use the drill. After considerable advice from friends and family and many unsuccessful attempts to correct the spin, another friend took the wheel away. He said he thought he knew someone who might be able to fix the wheel. When he brought it back, all problems were resolved. The wheel worked perfectly. I offered to pay my friend but he refused, saying he did not fix it. When I tried to find out who did fix the wheel, he would not tell me, told me not to worry, said it was all taken care of, and asked me to not mention his involvement to anyone. I thought his request strange, but I agreed.

A couple of nights after he returned the wheel, my doorbell rang. Since I lived in an upper-class neighborhood, I was not prepared for the appearance of the gang standing on my porch. There were four of them: one man in an expensive suit and three who would look more at home in the barrios and slums I visited as a social worker. Not waiting to be invited, they pushed past me into my living room. The suit moved into my personal space and demanded to know what I planned to do with the color/number wheel.

I was shocked! I could not imagine why he cared, but told him I planned to use the wheel at Aqua Fest. It was obvious that he did not believe me. As I explained about Little Fest, showed him my contract and the prizes I planned to use, his expression changed from hostile, to skeptical, to embarrassed amusement. When I finished my explanation, he told me it was OK to use the wheel as a children's game, but that I better not try anything else. In my ignorance I asked what else could I do

Me and My Color/Number Wheel

with the wheel? He looked at me as though I was daft, threatened me with violence if I tried anything else and left.

Now I was afraid! I had no idea what I was not supposed to do. I called my friend who took the wheel to be fixed. He came over immediately, looking as scared as I felt. He said, "The man who fixed your wheel works for the Mexican Mafia." He demanded to know if I gave the man who came to visit me his name. I assured him that I had not, told him what I said to the man, and asked him what the man meant. He explained that the Mexican Mafia runs color/number wheels as gambling devises for cash. This was of course illegal in Texas, but very profitable. They did not want any competition. He told me how lucky I was to be alive. Ignorance may be bliss, but if you are really naive (or just plain dumb,) it can get you killed!

The day before Aqua Fest started, I went to the bank to get change. We planned to charge a quarter for each game, so I asked for $800.00 in quarters. The teller asked if I wanted help but I said no. That is, until they picked me up off the floor where I fell when I tried to pick up the sack of change. Do you have any idea how much $800.00 in quarters weighs? Well, if you do, imagine $10,000.00 in quarters. That is how much I took in at the 10-day show, most of it in quarters. I had no idea carnival games could be so lucrative or that money could be so heavy.

When I returned to my day job, things had taken a turn for the worse. The contract to process Medicaid claims was awarded to a new company. The old company (which shall remain nameless because the owner is very well known) sued. They claimed my boss was out to get them because they had refused to hire him. They wanted me to testify for them. The Attorney General's office confiscated our files and we were not allowed to do any of our regular work.

In the meantime, my telephone rang off the hook with requests for me to run carnival games at various schools, fairs, and festivals. With dollar signs in my eyes from Aqua Fest, I followed the lyrics to the song, "Take This Job and Shove It" and leaped off the bureaucratic ship.

Before leaping, I thought about best and worst case scenarios. In the best case, I could have fun and get rich; in the worst case, I could lose everything, but the probability of that seemed slim. Thus I became "self-unemployed."

69 FUND RAISERS

Because I helped non-profit groups set up booths for Aqua Fest, a lot of people knew that I knew how to organize festivals and that I owned some carnival games. I received a number of requests to help PTA groups set up school carnivals and to bring my games. I didn't charge for my advice and I quickly learned that it was not cost-effective to run the games for profit for small groups since I had to rent a trailer to transport the games and hire people to run them. However the games were profitable for non-profit organizations because they had volunteer labor and men with trucks to schlep the heavy material around.

I ended up lending the equipment to groups like the Boy Scouts and then made small amounts of money selling them the carnival prizes they needed to run the games. Eventually, when I got out of the carnival game business, I donated my equipment to several non-profits as a charitable contribution and took a tax deduction for the value.

As to liquidating businesses, when I quit running the carnival games I should have sold the business rather than liquidate the assets but at the time I didn't know how to do that. Since then I've met people who make their money by starting businesses and then selling them for a profit.

70 DOG TAGS

While working on Aqua Fest, I met a true carny who owned carnival rides. He also owned a kiosk with an old dog tag machine. (You know, dog tags like the military uses.) Both the kiosk and the dog tag machine fascinated me. The kiosk had four sides with Plexiglas display cases and a striped canvas top. The dog tag machine was huge with spinning levers and gears and a keyboard like an old manual typewriter.

I thought the tags would be perfect for kids for identification, for medical emergency tags, for luggage, for keys, etc. The blank tags cost about five cents. He sold the finished tag for five dollars. He offered to sell me the machine and kiosk for $2,000, which he claimed I could earn back in one day. He also told me that I could schlep the kiosk and machine around by myself.

As it turned out, this was not the worst lie he told me. But the fact that I believed him shows how gullible I was. The machine alone weighed 500 pounds. It was a very good thing that I was an attractive young girl with lots of male friends who were willing to move the d** thing for me. Otherwise, it would still be sitting in my garage and would have earned me nothing.

In spite of the inconvenience of lugging this dinosaur around, the machine turned out to be a great moneymaker on two fronts. Because it was unique, it did well at fairs and festivals. It did paid for itself at the first show. It also became a great source of money in the mail. I made mail order blanks that I left on the counter of the kiosk when I did shows. For weeks after each show, I got orders in the mail.

However, my vision of what people would use the tags for was erroneous. Most tags were sold to kids who put things like "Sue-N-Ron 4 Ever" and "The Doors." If they did put names on the tags, it was to trade. Sue's tag went to Ron and Ron's tag went to Sue. I used to think about the possible mix-up in the emergency room and gave some thought to writing a book about things people put on dog tags.

When I got tired of lugging the dinosaur around, I put it out to pasture at a giant flea market between Dallas and Fort Worth. A guy who ran a shoe store asked for it, so I leased it to him. Later he was responsible for getting me a place at the Texas State Fair. However, that's another story.

Me, My Kiosk and Dog Tag Machine

71 LAW SUIT

When I leaped off the bureaucratic ship, I planned to support myself by running carnival games at local festivals. In fact, before I left my day job, I had bookings every week through the end of the year. Unfortunately, one month after I left my job and my health insurance policy, I fell and broke my ankle. The addition of a full ankle–to-hip cast made the already Herculean task of carrying my equipment around impossible. I had to cancel three months' bookings.

To make matters worse, the restaurant where the accident occurred refused to cover the doctor bills. As the accident was truly due to negligence on their part, I decided to sue. This charade taught me a lesson on perceptions. I asked friends who were with me at the time to testify.

When we compared memories, I was in for a shock. One remembered a "dark and stormy night," one remembered a "bright and sunny day." Others reported that the accident happened at the beginning of the evening before anyone had anything to drink (true). Or was it in the wee hours after tippling many a bottle? Several things were certain: it was very dark in the restaurant; there were stairs with no light, no guard rail, and a four-foot drop off. One of the waitresses fell in the same location and broke her leg the week before I did. We ended up in court.

In the pre-trial negotiations, the defense attorney persuaded my attorney to agree to limit the discussion to guard rails, then claimed we had no case because the code required hand rails, not guard rails. The judge declared a mistrial. After the mistrial, their attorney talked to the jury and bragged about the fact that the restaurant was liable, but hoped I would give up. I did not and eventually I received a settlement that covered not only my doctor's bill but the lost income.

The lessons I learned from this were mixed. Some people make a living filing suits. If they had paid the doctor's bills I would not have sued, and I would not choose to go this route again.

72 PHOTOS

An excellent way to make money is with a camera. One way to do it is as an artist through galleries or at the arts and craft shows. If you have talent and an interest in photography I highly recommend you try selling some of your work, for the ego boost if nothing else. However, if you're like most of us, with no particular talent or eye for pictures, you can still make money (and sometimes lots of it) with a camera. Look around you. Have you ever been to a fair, festival or event that had a booth where you stuck your head through a hole in a cut-out so you could have a souvenir picture taken? How about a riverboat cruse where they take your picture as you get on board and then sell them when you get off? Once upon a time, I did the souvenir picture thing at the New Braunfels Wurstfest (the German beer and sausage festival) with some friends who owned the setup. The usual take was about $2,000 per night.

I knew a couple that did this on riverboat cruises. The ship held 300 people, the tour lasted one hour, and the pictures cost $6.00 each. If everyone bought a picture, the potential was $1,800 per hour. Let's say they were all couples (150 potential sales) and only half (75) actually bought their picture. An income of $450 per hour is not bad. Look for a photo opportunity in your area and get busy.

Another way to make major money with a camera is the photo ID business. My dog tags and I once shared a booth at the Texas State Fair with a guy who did this. His gross was about $4K a night while I made between one and two thousand.

Originally I thought photo ID idea was great. However, most of the photos go to underage kids or illegal aliens and even if not illegal, than it's still a shady business. After the police threatened to arrest everyone in the booth if one more kid was caught with a fake ID, we asked for identification before taking a picture. Income for the remainder of that night was $20.00. You might want to check in your area to make sure a photo ID business is legal before you get started.

73 RODEO CIRCUIT

One of my most enjoyable, if bizarre, occupations was to follow the rodeo circuit with my dog tag machine. I had a friend who owned a t-shirt press and a button-making machine. You know, the kind that says "Kiss me I'm Irish." She had a friend named Flo who had a spin art kiosk. In her younger days, Flo worked the high wires at the circus and knew everyone inside and outside the ring. We joined forces to work the Texas rodeo circuit.

Our first show was the San Antonio Rodeo. Our Kiosk was set up between a guy who made fencing material and mats out of old tires and a guy who ran a booth where you played tic-tac-toe with a chicken (I'm not making this up, guys!) We did the Houston, Fort Worth, and Austin rodeos as well.

In Austin, the chicken guy was still on one side of me, but the other neighbor had a photography booth with old time dress-up clothes (another use for a camera.) His setup made sepia prints that put you back into the nineteenth century. The picture I made with the chicken guy and the photographer is still one of my prized possessions.

Rodeo Days

I made some money, met an incredible cast of characters and enjoyed myself. However, at heart I'm not a rodeo girl.

74 HAT TACKS & CLUB PINS

When I talked about carnival games, I explained that the carnival game business in Texas required consolation prizes as well as the winner's prize. If you wanted to make money from quarter games, it is important to keep costs down. To help the non-profit groups make more money on their carnivals, I went in search of cheaper prizes. This search eventually led me all the way through the normal distribution chain from manufacturer to retail, as well as down some of the side streets such as commodity brokers, damaged goods, and bankruptcy sales, and eventually to importing. I also learned what value-added benefit each step provided and came to understand why price is not always the most important consideration. For example, when I bought retail, I could buy one at a time. If I bought wholesale, I had to buy a larger quantity but the product was already packaged for re-sale. When I got back to the manufacturer, I had to buy by the gross and items were seldom packaged. Oh, what fun to put thousands of little consolation prizes into tiny plastic bags!

While doing the rodeo circuit I became enamored with the cloisonné pins and hat tacks sold at the rodeo. I tracked the source to a small company that imported the pins from a manufacturer in Taiwan. I learned that hat tacks (also called lapel pins) are popular with a wide range of groups such as the VFW, Elks and Eagles and with clubs like ski clubs, hot air balloon clubs, running clubs, and quilt guilds. I added lapel pins to my inventory and went in search of customers.

I had no trouble finding customers, but I did have trouble communicating with the manufacturer in Taiwan. Telex was used in the Dark Ages before the Internet and email. This meant words, not pictures. For a special order you had to describe what was wanted and hope the description didn't get lost in the translation from English to Chinese, which it usually did.

One of my first and best customers was the State VFW office. The VFW is a big user of pins, with flags and eagles being most popular. Each year the elected commander orders a custom pin to give out to favorites. The incoming commander wanted a Superman pin and tie bar for the state convention. The pin, a diamond shape with a big "S" in the center, was supposed to be about the size of my thumb and was needed before the convention.

Unfortunately, Murphy's Law strikes at the most inconvenient times. The day before the convention, the shipment of pins went awry and ended up in Chicago. I paid extra to have them shipped same-day delivery. They arrived all right, but the translation from English to Chinese failed. The pin was a diamond with an "S" all right, but instead of being small it was about ½ inch tall and three inches wide with very, very sharp points. Anyone wearing that tie bar had better be into body piercing. Also, they were not individually packaged as requested. The Commander was not impressed. Since the banquet was that evening, there was nothing that could be done in time. I gave him the awful things, told him there would be no charge and that I would re-order the pins.

He handled it better than I would have. That is until Murphy struck again. The second pin came in looking much like the first except this time the pin was ½ wide and three inches tall! The sharp points were still there and the pins should have come with a warning not to sit down or bend over while wearing one of the lethal things.

This time the Commander did not take it well. In fact, I congratulated myself on getting out of there alive. Once again I promised to re-order, but he told me what I could do with the pins and took his business elsewhere. I still have some of the pins among my souvenirs.

75 KIOSK

You know the kiosks that march down the center of all shopping malls these days? Well, once upon a time there was no such thing. Mall aisles were wide and empty, the better to see the merchandise displayed in the store windows. Seeing the empty space gave me a vision of a new way to make money.

As you may recall from the section on dog tags, I was the proud possessor of one four-sided kiosk with Plexiglas display cases and a striped canvas top. I also had a large and miscellaneous quantity of carnival prizes and a dog tag machine. Running carnival games is a seasonal occupation. At Christmas time, the equipment and prizes were doing nothing but taking up space in my garage.

I went to see the local mall manager about renting space in the aisle for my kiosk. At first, the manager was not receptive to the idea. He was afraid that the store owners would not welcome the competition. I pointed out that what I had to sell (dog tags, hat tacks and stocking stuffers) was not available at the mall. I suggested we visit the surrounding stores and ask the owners if they had any objection. As none did, I rented cheap space in the center aisle and set up for business as the first kiosk in the mall. For good measure and to attract attention, I added helium balloons to my mix of products for sale and did a booming business for Christmas.

After my successful season, the manager realized a new source of income. The mall where I had my kiosk blossomed with kiosks. This trend was picked up by other malls in the area. Now, I cannot claim that my great idea resulted in the proliferation of mall kiosks across the United States. However, I do know my kiosk set a trend in my town. So much so that the next Christmas I found no room at the inn (I mean mall) for my own kiosk.

76 FAIRS & FOOD

After reading # 68 Carnival Games through # 74 Kiosk you will realize that I spent a good deal of my time at fairs, festivals, and shows, running games, making dog tags, and finding locations to sell carnival stuff. At some shows, what I had sold well. At others, I had plenty of time to observe the crowd and see what was going on in other booths. What I noticed was that food was the one thing that sold at all the events. Always on the lookout for a better product, I decided to try food.

My first attempt at food sales was the Fourth of July. I bought three bottles of syrup (lime, strawberry and grape) with pump tops and cups from a food wholesaler. Then I filled an ice chest with snow cone ice from an ice house and borrowed a grocery cart from the local supermarket. With supplies in hand, I went to the local Fourth of July parade. I sold the cones for $1.00 with a cost per cone of three cents. Within an hour I made $50.00. With that experience in hand, I took the grocery cart back to the store and ordered a snow cone machine.

That machine in now long gone, but now that I am retired I am seriously thinking of getting another snow cone machine. This is surely one way you can make extra money with little upfront cost and on your own schedule. Of course today, I'll have to explore health department and licensing requirements. This might put the cost per cone considerably higher than it was in the Dark Ages.

My next attempt was turkey legs, the kind they sell at Renaissance festivals. I bought boxes of frozen turkey legs from a smoke house and rented a large barbecue pit on wheels. At a one-day street festival in Austin, I sold $2,000 dollars' worth of turkey legs.

In # 73 Rodeo Circuit, I mentioned a friend of mine who had a t-shirt press and a button machine. This same friend had a booth at a place call Canton where she and her husband sold sausage on a stick. Since the 1800s, Canton has been the home of the largest flea market in Texas (and maybe the world, for all I know.) I've been there a number of times and never covered the whole grounds.

The First Monday Market was open once a month from Sunday to Monday. The day before the market, my friend and her husband loaded their mobile home with boxes of frozen sausage, beer, and whatever friends wanted to go along. For the next couple of days we would take turns sitting in the mobile home, drinking beer, selling sausage, or roaming the flea market. While a great time was had by all, my friend and her husband made a couple of thousand dollars extra once every month. In my book, not a bad deal if you can get it!

After my success with the turkey legs at the street festival, I decided to tackle Canton. The first problem was the lack of a mobile home. I solved that problem with money: I rented a house trailer. Turkey legs take up more space than sausage and of course I had to have the barbecue pit (also rented.) By the time I got the rented barbecue pit hitched to the rented trailer, hitched to my tiny Honda Accord, filled with friends and boxes of turkey legs, we looked like we should be headed to the circus rather than to a flea market. "Onward through the fog," I always say.

You have probably heard that the three most important things in real estate are location, location, location. Well, the same thing applies to booths at fairs and festivals. When we got to Canton, I found my booth located at the very back of the market, up against a fence surrounded by cows. As I said, Canton was so big that I had been there several times and never covered the whole ground. This meant I had never made it back as far as my booth, and neither did most of the crowd. By the end of the market, I was down about $2,000 and was the proud owner of multiple boxes of rapidly defrosting turkey legs.

When I returned to Austin, I went to a frozen food locker to rent a box for my turkey legs. Unfortunately the boxes for home rental held only two of my many, many boxes. I needed a commercial flat which was not available. After some hard negotiating and tears, I managed to talk the owner of the lockers into renting me space in a commercial flat. This temporarily solved the problem of the defrosting turkey legs. My long-term solution was to donate the legs to the Rape Crisis Center for them to sell at a festival to raise money for the center.

77 BARTER & # 78 BROKER

I joined a barter club in 1980, after I became self-unemployed. In these days of Craig's List, eBay, Amazon and Bitcoins, I don't know how popular barter clubs are, but in my day they were very popular among the entrepreneurial set and the unemployed. For those of you who have never encountered a barter club, the concept is that instead of using cash, you trade your goods or services with other club members for their goods or services. This of course is a very old concept of the human race that predates the invention of money. Money after all is simply a portable stand-in for all the goods and services in the world.

The advantage of using money is that you don't have to find someone who wants what you have and has what you want. Without using money, barter clubs circumvent this problem by using some form of point system. If I want something another member has but they don't want what I have they can give me what I want and get points that can be traded with other members. In this manner, barter clubs proved an alternative currency and another way for people without money to get what they want.

Barter clubs work best for service-providers such as plumbers, electricians and hairdressers or for people who sell necessary products like food and clothing. In my case, my products were paintings, stained glass, dog tags and carnival prizes. My services were reading palms and running carnival games. Neither my products nor services were in high demand in the barter world. However, as a member I was introduced to a whole new world of trade, the brokerage business.

According to Wikipedia, "A broker is an individual or party (brokerage firm) that arranges transactions between a buyer and a seller for a commission when the deal is executed...." Wikipedia list 34 types of brokers. The type of brokerage to which I was introduced wasn't on the list. To me the most appropriate title would be Freelance Broker. Either you find someone who has something to sell and you try to find a buyer or you find someone who wants to buy something and you try to find a seller. I'm sure freelance brokers still exist but prior to the Internet there was a greater need for such a service and quite an extensive network of freelance brokers.

My first sale as a freelance broker was for sucker rods. What are sucker rods you might ask? According to Wikipedia: "A sucker rod is a steel rod, typically between 25 and 30 feet (7 to 9 meters) in length, and threaded at both ends, used in the oil industry ..."

You might also wonder how I happened to know about sucker rods. The truth is, I didn't. My father was in the oil business. Through a fortuitous accident I overheard a conversation between my dad and another oil man. Drilling a well had to be stopped because a steel strike resulted in a shortage of sucker rods. At the time I had no idea what a sucker rod was, but one of my broker contacts mentioned that he had a source for sucker rods. I mentioned that I had a prospective buyer and the end result was a commission for selling sucker rods.

Over time I sold an assortment of things, such as a shipment of chewing gum and one of ceiling fans. A lot of the merchandise came from insurance companies; when an insurance company pays a claim for a shipment damaged in transit, the insurance company owns the merchandise. Some came from companies going out of business and some from individuals. An attorney friend accepted some gem stone jewelry as payment for services and asked me to sell them for him. The largest sale I almost made was for an airplane. I found a buyer but another broker got there first. I mention this because this particular deal led to a job offer to be a registered broker for an import company.

As a freelance broker you not only need to match buyer and seller, but you also need to negotiate your commission and protect yourself to make sure you don't get cut out of the deal. Good faith and handshakes don't necessarily work. The primary difference between a freelance broker and a registered broker is that as a registered broker the percentage of your commission is already established and you have a legally enforceable contract with the seller or the buyer. It's like being a salesman for a company without being an employee.

79 IMPORTS

The import firm was a startup business run by two retired federal employees who had worked for U.S. Customs. I assumed that they knew what they were doing as they were former executives. However, this assumption proved to be wrong, as you will see as this story unfolds. (Remember "to assume makes an ass of u and me"?)

In my new job, the import company gave me a list of the merchandise they had imported and of the type of merchandise they could import. When I found a buyer I would take the specifics to the company and they would deliver the goods or make arrangements to import the item. For example, my first sale was for a shipment of briefcases the company had already imported.

The briefcases looked really great. Unfortunately the workmanship turned out to be really shoddy. When customers returned them to the store, the store owner expected a refund from me. I expected the import company would cover the loss, but my assumption turned out to be false. The store owner was not a happy camper and would certainly not buy anything else from me. For my part I learned something new about product guarantees.

My second sale was for baseball uniforms for a Little League team. The import company had to make arrangements to import these. The group was really happy with the price I quoted, but they were really unhappy when it turned out that the uniforms were held up in Customs because the quota for importing cotton goods from the country of origin had already been exceeded. I recovered from this one by arranging a deal to have the uniforms delivered to a free trade zone in San Antonio, Texas, where the logos were embroidered on the uniforms. That qualified them for import but at an additional cost to me and not in time for the first game. There were a lot of unhappy kids and moms mad at me over that one. I lost money on the deal and learned something about import quotas that I assumed the import company knew. There's that word "assume" again.

My last deal for the import company had to do with video games, the kind they have at video parlors. The company sent me a flyer listing some video game machines they had imported. It turned out the games were very popular and hard to come by. I found several parties interested in buying the games, but something didn't seem right to me. Considering my experience with the import quotas, I decided to check with Customs before I placed an order for the machines. This time the problem wasn't quotas, it was copyrights. The machines were knock-offs, illegal copies of licensed games. If I sold them I could be jailed for copyright infringement.

When I gave this information to the import company, they were very upset because it meant they would lose the money they had spent buying the machines. I was happy because this time I wasn't on the hook. I decided to get out of the import business before I lost my shirt or ended up in jail.

The global lesion I learned from this adventure is that price is not the only consideration in buying and selling. The lesson for you is that if you plan to sell something for a company, make sure the company knows what it is doing and backs its product before you waste your time and reputation.

80 WINDOW WASHER

This was a short-lived job but worth mentioning here because it is a quick way to earn some money and a great business opportunity for someone.

A friend of mine called and asked if I could help her. She need some money immediately and had heard that I knew some ways to make money in a hurry. As it turned out, one of the things I had been thinking about was washing windows. My windows needed washing but I had not found anyone willing to do the work. I found commercial window washers but could not find anyone willing to wash residential windows. I thought this problem was not unique to me but really didn't know. I suggested that we give window washing a try.

The next day we gathered window washing supplies and started knocking on doors in my neighborhood. I lived in an older part of town and was surrounded by elderly neighbors. I reasoned that they were probably a good market for window washing services. Boy, was I right! My friend and I were immediately hired to wash windows at several houses. We worked a long hard day and returned to my house with the money my friend needed.

As we discussed the day's results and the overwhelming response, we realized that there was a business opportunity here. We could set up a residential window-washing business. We could line up the jobs and hire people to do the work. After outlining a rudimentary business plan, she and I realized that the opportunity was certainly there, but that neither one of us really wanted to run a window-washing business.

The need still exists. I know, because recently a neighbor found an individual who washes residential windows. Unfortunately he lives in another town. He has so much work in his own town that the only way he would come to wash her windows was if she could guarantee two houses. I was more than happy to agree. The man did an excellent job and earned $700.00 for a day's work. At that rate I think a business opportunity still exists.

81 PIANO BAR

If you remember, I had had a part-time job as a bartender. The year was 1968; I was 26 at that time and really enjoyed the job. Rolling the clock forward to 1982 when I was 40, I decided to get out of the carnival game business and get into real estate. This meant that I had to go back to school to get a real estate license and needed to find some way to support myself while I changed careers.

The first thing I did was expand my Enterprising Artist business by accepting commissions for both paintings and stained glass. I was still doing art shows and worked with a couple of home builders on a regular basis, so I began advertising for commissions. Stained glass is very time-consuming so soon I had more work than time.

One of the big jobs I accepted was to do a set of large stained glass windows with a Texas theme for my neighbors. When I realized I was overbooked I explained to the neighbors that they would still get the windows but the job would take longer than my original estimate. I also mentioned that I need to find a part-time job to support myself while I was taking classes. They were very understanding about the windows and offered a solution for my immediate money needs, a part-time job as a cocktail waitress at a piano bar they frequented. They took me to the bar and introduced me to the owner. She said the job required a lot of energy and was skeptical about my age, but agreed to give me a try because my neighbors were good customers.

The piano bar was much like my first bar. The customers were mostly nice and the money was good. However, the owner was right to be skeptical about my age. Though I wouldn't let her know, being out of shape the first few weeks nearly killed me. Even after I got used to standing on my feet for hours, I still hurt. Consequently, though, I was happy to get the job; I was happier still to leave it when my real estate career was established.

Whenever I see an older woman working as a waitress I think about my experience and am ever so grateful that I didn't have to do that forever; I make sure to tip them as generously as possible.

82 HOUSE NUMBERS

I had a friend who didn't seem to have a job but always had money. I thought he might be a drug dealer but didn't think it would be polite to ask. However, when I really needed money, he volunteered his secret. He painted house numbers on curbs. He said he usually made $125 -$150 a day when he worked. $125 a day is $15.63 an hour for an eight-hour day. That might not sound like much now, but in 1983 minimum wage was $3.25 an hour. $125.00 for a day's work was a veritable fortune and he told me he only worked an average of four hours a day when he wanted money.

Here's how it works: Go to a hobby or office supply business and buy a roll of masking tape, spray paint and a set of individual number templates. (The rubber mat type works best.) Make a flyer stating that you will be in the neighborhood on a specific date to paint house numbers on curbs. Give some reasons why house numbers on curbs are a good thing: EMS and firemen can find your house when you need them and it helps your friends find you. Include a price and instructions to tape this flyer to their door if they want you to paint their house number. Tell them to include an envelope with payment if they will not be home or want the number but don't want you to bother them. Distribute the flyers in the selected neighborhood. Return on the specified date and look for flyers taped to doors. Collect your payment, then tape the correct number templates to the curb and spray paint them.

I tried this and it worked. You probably won't get rich on this one but it is a great way to earn some fast money. It's also a great way for a non-profit to earn money. I suggested it to my volunteer fire company. When they sent out their appeal for donations they included information about house numbers. My community doesn't have curbs but it does have street-side mail boxes, so they ordered reflective signs and attached them to the boxes.

83 REMODELER

My house in Austin was built in 1932. I bought it in 1972 and remodeled it to be my home forever. Then my father passed away and my mother announced that she planned to move to be closer to one of her daughters. I decided to add a mother-in-law apartment to the house so she would have a place to live should she decide to move to Austin.

I wanted to add an apartment behind the garage like my neighbor had done but discovered setback problems. The prior owner of my house sold some of the property to the neighbor so they could build their garage apartment but neglected to move the fence or fig tree. Therefore I did not have the space required by the city to do what I wanted there. I moved on to plans to add a second story to my house and set it up as a separate apartment with a conversion option.

As it was an old pier and beam house, I brought in a structural engineer to determine if the house could support a second floor and was assured that my architectural plans would work. Unfortunately I hired as a contractor a "friend" named John who viewed architectural plans as suggestions instead of requirements and wouldn't hire crews to do work he could do.

The first thing to go was my roof, leaving my whole house exposed to the elements. Next he and is partner spent six weeks hand building the structural frame for a wooden castle on top of my house. Paying themselves executive wages, they quickly ran through the contracted price of $24,000, which was the cost of the original house, and then asked for more money.

I went to the bank to increase the home equity loan. The lender said, "You have a $70,000 line of credit but we can't give you more money until you complete what we already paid for." When I reported this fact to the contractor he said that if he didn't get paid, he wouldn't work. From his perspective the contract price was just an estimate and he did not understand my reluctance to pay more. After all, they had worked there every day.

I consulted an attorney. He verified that the contractor was so poor he did not have a pot to pee in (A colorful Texas colloquial meaning he was judgment-proof because he had no money or assets.) He went on to say, "Little Lady, if you had a husband you would not be in this fix." I had to agree with him but it didn't help me get out of the mess.

I returned home to my roofless house in near-total despair. What in the world was I to do now!? No money and no roof heading into fall. As I carried on with my pity party, a friend of mine came by and offered a solution. She said: "Why don't you have a roofing party?" At first I thought she was crazy. Who in the world would want to come to a party to roof my house?

She pointed out that I gave fabulous parties that everyone wanted to attend, and that some of my friends were in construction and knew how to do things, while others wanted to learn. She said that the friends who just wanted to party would come also and provide manual labor if asked. I thought a minute and realized she was right. I didn't know anything about construction but I did know how to put on a party. In any case it was worth the risk. At worst, I wouldn't get any work done but we'd still have a party.

Still skeptical, I decided to give it a try. It worked just as my friend predicted. I set up the downstairs as a normal party and bought building supplies for upstairs. I invited everyone I knew and gave them permission to bring friends. About 75 people showed up to work and/or party. Much to my surprise, my ex-contractor also showed up with some construction friends. Before long, everything was organized and humming along. Some worked, some learned, some provided support and everyone partied. By the end of the party, most of the roof was framed and everyone wanted to know when the next party was. They picked up and put away everything before they left.

At the end of that day I realized I finally learned the secret of how to get people to work for me: 1) Create an environment where people want to do what you want them to do or at least where they want to be. 2) Tell them what you want done. 3) Don't tell them how to do it, unless asked. 4) Give them permission to do what they want to do. 5)

Get out of the way and let them do it. 6) Provide support when asked and let them know how much you appreciate what they are doing for you. Remember Camp Sylvania? At some level, I had known this secret since age six.

With the labor needs tentatively handled, I realized my part was to figure out how to get the money to provide building and party supplies, no small feat when I considered the magnitude of the task. I sat down to make plans for more parties and began making lists of possible ways to earn money. Without regard to all the "yes buts" in my mind, I visualized options and made lists of possibilities, then in the light of day I viewed the list for practicality and preference and followed up on the ones that looked possible. For example, one idea was to bake and sell cookies at the mall (this was before anyone ever heard of Mrs. Fields or Great American Cookies.) I reasoned the smell of baking cookies would draw people in. I also wanted to hire young people dressed in 19th century attire and give them baskets of cookies to sell on the street. This really was a good idea, but on the practical side the cost of the equipment was prohibitive and health department obstacles made it difficult. Most of the ideas I did pursue are included here in this book.

With more framing, roofing, insulation, sheet rocking, siding, flooring and painting parties, I got a roof over my head and finished the upstairs within a year. Unfortunately the house's exposure through the preceding spring, summer, fall, and winter meant that all the rooms downstairs needed repair. When I thought all was said and done, I notices cracks appearing in the walls. A call to a structural engineer revealed that the contractors framing did not followed the architect's plans; instead he had added twice the weight to the addition, thus exceeding the weight-bearing load of the original house.

The whole house had to be jacked up and the pier and beam foundation reinforced. This turned out to be a good thing, though, because during the construction the gas line that fed the furnace developed a small leak and gas was accumulating under the house.

With time and a spark my whole house would have blown sky high, probably with me in it.

Over the years I've kept my guardian angel busy keeping me alive. I do appreciate it, but sometime, to get my attention, a gentle whisper in the ear might be preferable to hitting me over the head with two by four.

In the end my mother moved to Fort Worth to be with my younger sister and I rented the apartment. I will be forever grateful to all my friends and suppliers who saved me from a total disaster and left me with a jewel of a house. As a footnote I would like to say that, my contractor, never understood what he did wrong. Several friends tried the method I used to remodel their homes. I tried to help them, but none succeeded. I guess they didn't know how to throw a party.

84 RENTAL PROPERTY

When my mother moved to Fort Worth instead of Austin, I was left with a vacant furnished apartment. The rental income from the apartment would pay my mortgage, so I decided to become a landlady.

Historically, owning rental property is a proven route to riches. I say historically, because with today's fluctuation in property values, owning rentals can be a route either to riches or to the poor house. There are several factors that make rental property attractive: 1) Because of inflation, the value of property tends to increases over time. Historically the rate of increase was about 8%, which made property a good investment; 2) Today most people do not pay cash for homes, they pay a down payment equal to 5%, 10%, or 20% of the price. However inflation applies to the total price of the property, not the down payment; 3) Your tenant pays the mortgage or most of it; 4) The costs of owning rental property plus depreciation are tax deductible. In spite of the risks and many downsides of owning rental property, it's still a pretty good deal.

My first experience as a landlady taught me something about the risks and downsides of owning rental property. My first mistake was to rent the place to two young men who turned out to be college students with girlfriends and lots of buddies who moved in shortly after the boys moved in.

Aside from the noise level, the first problem became apparent when the washing machine and dryer ran continually. From the volume of laundry I think the whole college must have been using my machines.

The next problem surfaced when I got my first utility bill. (Note: Never include utilities with rent.) I went upstairs to talk to the boys, but nobody answered my knock. The door was open, so I stepped inside and was shocked by what I saw. The new carpet had red wine stains and burned holes from cigarettes. A chair, two lamps and a stained glass chandelier were broken. In the bathroom, both the fiberglass tub and sink had cigarette burns and a hole had been punched in the door. The first bedroom obviously had a female occupant and several futons had been moved into the second bedroom. One was occupied by a boy who was not my tenant. I woke him up and asked him what he was doing there. He said "I live here." (Note: Be sure the lease includes who can live there.)

I left the apartment in a state of shock. How could so much damage happen in one month! I knew I had to do something so I called the Austin Tenants' Council to determine what I could do legally. Much to my dismay, I learned that the eviction process could take six to nine months. By that time the whole apartment would be trashed. Somehow I had to get the boys to move voluntarily.

I solved the problem by scheduling a meeting with my tenants. I gave them a list of the damage done to the apartment and a second list of all the ways they violated their lease. Then I told them that unless they voluntarily moved, I would have to file for eviction and report their behavior to the University of Texas. Next I said: "If you move out immediately, I will refund your deposit and the last month's rent. If you don't move out immediately, I will keep your money and file for eviction." They moved out the next week.

After that experience I read a number of books on how to manage rental property. All the books provided good advice, but one book in particular stated that the key to successful management was to get a good tenant and provided a method to screen prospects for the qualities you want in a tenant. The first step is to determine the qualities you want. What I wanted was a tenant who: Would pay rent on time; Take care of the property as if it were his or her own, and; Not call me at 0' dark thirty to make repairs.

The second step is to provide incentives for the behavior you want. The author suggested that the most effective incentive was to offer a discount on the rent. With that advice in hand, when a prospect called I stated how much the rent was, then offered a $50.00 a month discount provided the tenant would: Pay rent by the first of the month; Make arrangements for any repairs, and; Be responsible for the first $50.00 of any necessary repair

The response amazed me. Only one in ten understood the offer. Most callers were angry that I expected them to make arrangements for repairs or pay for the first $50. They said that was my job. Some felt it shouldn't matter when they paid rent as long as they paid. Several argued that if I was willing to take $50.00 less for the rent I should charge $50.00 less without expecting the tenant to do anything. These were the tenants that I did not want. The ones who understood the offer and considered it to be a good deal were the tenants I wanted.

For the rest of my tenure as a landlady I used this approach to screen prospects and had no further problem tenants. In fact when I needed to sell my rentals, I sold most of them to the tenants. To make it easier for them to buy, I carried the mortgages. That gave me a higher interest rate than I would have made by getting cash and putting the money in the bank and gave me monthly income which I needed.

85 REAL ESTATE

There were two reasons I wanted to get into real estate. When my first husband went to medical school, I expected him to graduate and get rich practicing medicine. I planned to get into real estate and buy the town, or at least buy rental property. Since he stayed in school and didn't get rich until long after I left, I abandoned that plan but had not forgotten it. The second reason was that Austin, Texas, was chosen as the headquarters for a high tech consortium that included all the major players such as IBM, Lockheed, Motorola, and Texas Instruments. This turned Austin into a boom town with the number one real estate market in the world. I saw the boom coming and decided to get out of carnival games into real estate and ride the wave to riches.

Real estate was one of the best and worst jobs I've had. One of the good things about the real estate profession is that you don't have to have money to make money. When I got my real estate license, the first thing I did was put my own house on the market. If you will remember, the house was supposed to be my home forever. However, when I added the second story, I turned my little cottage into a McMansion that no longer met my needs.

In 1972, I bought the property for $24,000. In 1982, after remodel, it appraised for $250,000. I thought the increase in value was a result of the remodeling work I had done. This meant I could net enough from the sale of my house to buy a new home and still have money left over to buy other houses to remodel and sell. My game plan changed from selling real estate to selling real estate and remodeling houses.

When I looked for a replacement home to remodel I discovered the going rate for comparable homes was around $90,000. "How could this be?" I wondered. The answer turned out to be inflation. A $24,000 home purchased in 1972 cost $89,000 in 1982. Still this left a hefty margin for profit. I used part of the money from the sale of the house to put a down payment on and remodel my new home, bought another house to remodel and sell, and bought my first rental house so I could offset taxes with depreciation. I was on my way to becoming rich.

One of the most interesting things I did as a realtor was to help the residents of a down and out trailer park form a co-op to buy the park from the cocaine-addicted owner. The social worker in me enjoyed helping the people reach their goal and the realtor in me got a listing and sale in a million-dollar deal. That story could make a book by itself.

From 1980 to 1984 the market was booming. I got my broker's license, set up my own company, continued the remodels, bought

rental houses and got into developing raw land. By December, 1984, I was a millionaire on paper and thought I was set for life. It was costing me $125,000 to keep my home, business and properties afloat.

I knew that the real estate boom could not last forever, so my game plan was to complete all development projects before the boom ended. I had set money aside so that when the crash came, I could buy rental property and retire to live off my rentals. At that time I was involved in developing a sub-division, building a Section 8 apartment building, remodeling a house, and sub-dividing an inter-city lot. All projects were scheduled to be completed by fall of 1985. Unfortunately the crash came in January, 1985.

Diana Dunaway
Real Estate Broker

Some of you might remember having property values affected by the savings and loan crisis of the

144

'80s and '90s. The S&L crisis hit Austin in January, 1986, when the FDIC auditors marched into Austin to audit the local savings and loans.

There were many causes of the S&L debacle, including Reagan era tax law changes that adversely affected the value of property, but this story is about how to make money, not how to lose it. If you're really interested, Google "savings and loan crisis and Reagan administration scandals." The end result was called the worst scandal in U.S. history, with the government takeover of 747 out of 3,234 S&Ls in the country at a cost to taxpayers of $160 billion. (Note: Some recent failures such as the collapse of the financial markets in the first decade of the 21st century might eclipse the S&L crisis, but by then I had a job and a husband so except for a delayed retirement, I was all right.)

In Texas, we lost 40% to 60% of the equity value in property. The Texas governor and lieutenant governor both filed for personal bankruptcy and I lost my shirt. From 1985 to 1987, I lived with severe anxiety and depression as I tried everything I could think of to stay afloat.

First I tried working harder, then smarter, then focused on reducing expenses. It took me three years to lose everything I spent my life accumulating: my business, my investments, rental property, savings and retirement.

The last asset to go was my home. I paid the house payment as long as I could by taking cash advances from Master Card and Visa (a big mistake!) By the time I was three months in arrears and had received my first foreclosure notice, the mortgage was under water. At that time, the market value of the house was $125,000 and the mortgage was $135,000. This meant that I would either have to sell the house for more that it was worth or take money that I did not have to closing to pay off the mortgage. The only thing I had going for me was an 8% mortgage when the current rate was 12%. If the loan could be assumed, I could sell the house for the mortgage amount and show the buyer how this would save them money.

To keep my house from foreclosure I called my lender at the savings and loan and asked if they would help me sell the house by making my loan assumable. The lender, who was a friend of mine, said, "It is not to the bank's advantage to help you sell the house." He explained that if they foreclosed, they would own a house worth $125,000 plus they would collect $47,000 from the private mortgage insurance (PMI) on the house. I said, "Let me get this straight. If you foreclose, you collect the PMI that I paid for plus you get my house?" He said, "Yes, and the PMI Company will sue you to recover their money." Somehow this didn't seem right.

The next thing I did was call the private mortgage insurance company to ask for their help. I told the agent, "I am about to lose my home and if I do, you will lose $47,000." I told him about my conversation with the loan officer and my plan to market the house if the loan could be assumed. I asked the agent to help me negotiate with the savings and loan to make the loan assumable and to agree to pay any shortfall at closing if I found a buyer. He agreed.

With help from the agent, Franklin agreed to modify the loan and the private mortgage company agreed to pay the past due payments and closing costs. I found a buyer and sold the house.

With the house sold, with no place to go and no money, my next issue was how to deal with all the stuff I accumulated. The first thing I did was sort the things in the house into piles. My house was a gathering place for friends so the first pile was other people's things to be returned. The next pile was functional things such as dishes, silverware, pots and pans, and clothing, followed by a pile of functional but expendable things such as my Queen Anne dining room table and chairs, oriental carpets, lamps and books. Next came a pile of pretty but non-functional things such as paintings, stained glass and knickknacks. Then I asked myself why I had acquired each object to determine if I had any emotional attachment to it. This process resulted in two more stacks, things for a garage sale and things to give away. Among other things, I donated 40 boxes of books to the library.

A friend offered to lend me an empty garage in a condo she owned to store things; that was a godsend but the garage was without air conditioning. I was reluctant to store such things as antiques, oil paintings and oriental carpets there. I solved this problem by inviting friends to come and take anything they wanted home on "long-term, temporary loan," to be returned if I ever had need of them and to be kept if I never got my act back together.

After the garage sale, I called the Salvation Army and made arrangements with them to carry off the remainder. In this manner I sold, stored, gave away, and distributed my prize possessions (including my dogs) to friends, and put myself in survival mode: only me and my car.

At that point, I felt a tremendous weight lift off my shoulders and realized that from 1985 to1987 I lived under a cloud of fear, anxiety and depression as my world fall apart. Once everything I spent my life working for was finally gone, instead of feeling like a failure, I felt happy. In fact so happy that a group of new friends who had only known me as depressed thought I was having a nervous breakdown and tried to have me committed.

Apparently an involuntary commitment takes several signatures so they were calling my friends asking them to sign. My phone ran off the hook as friends called to warning me. I didn't think I was crazy, but just in case, I went to my college roommate's house, explained what was going on, and asked if I could stay with her for a few days. I said, "If you think I'm crazy, I'll committee myself."

A few days later she said, "Diana, you are not crazy. They just don't know you. You have returned to your normal optimistic self." It was then that I realized that the fear, anxiety and depression I felt from 1985 to 1987 was what was crazy. My only failure was to enjoy. During that period I always had a roof over my head, I always had friends and I always had food. The truth is that if you have those things, you have everything you need.

In 1987, I literally became a bag lady with a mink coat, and I would have been on the street except for the charity of friends who took me in and helped me recover. I think the story of how I maneuvered through the downtime between 1985 and 1987 would make interesting reading but again this is a story of gain, not loss. In July, 1987, owing $25,000 to Master Card and Visa, I moved out of my lovely home into a trailer at a fireworks stand.

As a footnote to this story I wanted to mention that after I moved out of the house, the Salvation Army called to tell me that, when they came to pick up the stuff I intended to donate, the garage was empty. I told my yard man that he could have the lawn mower and other gardening things, so I assumed that he took it all and gave the mystery no additional thought.

86 HOT AIR BALLOONS

I want to include this section for three reasons. First, being a homeless bag lady does not mean you can't have fun. Second, this is another example of how to get what you want for no money, and third, there is a job opportunity here for someone (unfortunately not me.)

When you don't have a job, what you do have is time. I   joined   a hot air balloon club in Austin, Texas, in 1987. Flying hot air balloons can be a life-or-death sport and the only reason to fly them is fun. It's a team sport as the pilot needs crew to get the balloon in the air, to land it, and take it down. With the exception of some commercial pilots, balloonists use volunteer crew. The best pilots know how to manage people and make it fun. This includes giving crew free flights and taking them out to eat, not to mention the free champagne that is obligatory at the end of each flight.

Why champagne? As the story goes, the Montgolfier brothers who invented hot air balloons ran into trouble when they landed in farmers' fields. Since the farmers had never seen anything like the balloon, they viewed the brothers as extraterrestrials and tended to take after them with pitchforks. To prove they were earthlings, the brothers carried French champagne to share with the pitchfork-wielding farmers.

There are balloon festivals all over the country, such as the Albuquerque International Balloon Festival, the largest in the world. Most pilots take their crews with them and pay their expenses. In addition, festivals and local pilots schedule parties and special activities for visiting pilots and their crews. This means that crew members not only fly for free and get free admission to the festivals, but they are also invited to all the parties. This package deal costs a bundle if you have to pay for it.

The first time I went to the Albuquerque Festival, I crewed for Gerry Graff, the pilot who won the festival that year; the prize was a new hot air balloon. Gerry knew all the pilots and introduced us to many of them. As the largest balloon festival in America, the Albuquerque event includes many specialty balloons sponsored by companies. I met the woman who flew the Coca Cola balloon. In addition to the red balloon, she had a red Coca Cola van and six good-looking young men dressed in matching red uniforms. I learned that Coca Cola paid to fly them to festivals not only around the country but around the world. I had a new role model and new career goal. I would get a hot air balloon pilot's license and a commercial sponsor.

When I returned home I enrolled in ground school, made arrangements for a flight instructor, and talked to Gerry about buying his old balloon, a Raven with a rainbow design. I got a private pilot's license, but my world fell apart before I bought the balloon and had enough flight time to get a commercial license. However, I continued to crew for other pilots and went to several festivals around the country for free.

87 FIRE WORKS STAND

You might wonder how a former millionaire ended up living in a trailer and running a fireworks stand. Quite by accident, I assure you. Before I became a bag lady, one of my agents asked me to sign for a fireworks stand for him. He explained that he did not have the credit rating to qualify. I agreed to sign, and by the time July rolled around, he had a job in another town and I inherited the fireworks stand. This turned out to be a good thing because at the time I had nowhere else to go and no money to go anywhere.

When I agreed to take on the fireworks stand, I was filled with fear and trepidation. I had a mental image of myself all alone in a stand located on a street or highway in a bad part of town. Since I had nowhere else to sleep, I imagined myself in a sleeping bag on the floor of the stand without air conditioning or bathroom. How would I feed myself and attend to other bodily functions?

As it turned out none of my fears came to be. First, a friend of mine owned an RV which he hoped to sell. He offered to let me use the RV if I would put a-for-sale sign on it and show it to any prospective buyers. Next, the fireworks company assigned me the stand located in their lighted, patrolled parking lot and offered to let me use their restroom facilities. As to being alone, several friends offered to help me sell fireworks and others showed up with food. Soon the stand resembled one of my parties with a continual stream of people in and out and no one wanting to leave. In fact so many people stayed overnight, I found myself wishing to be alone.

One night after the stand closed several of us got into a mock battle where we shot Roman candles at each other and tossed firecrackers. We all thought it was great fun. The next day we heard about a stand down the road that blew up. It seems the stand owners were having a mock battle and one of the Roman candles hit the stand and set it on fire. No one was hurt because the owners were outside the stand. The person telling us about the blowup talked about how stupid they were and how lucky to be alive. We exchanged looks but didn't say anything and realized we were even luckier.

After paying for the fireworks and paying the friends who wanted to be paid, I netted $1,500.00 from the stand and a Black Cat firecracker poster I always meant to frame. When I got a buyer for the RV, another friend offered to let me move into a vacant office suite he owned, so I had somewhere to go. The suite had a bathroom but no tub. I solved that problem by joining the gym at the Y, where there was a shower.

Black Cat Poster

88 MORTGAGE NOTES

As it turned out, the $1,500.00 I made at the fireworks stand was the only money I made from the end of July to the first of November. I survived through my friend's loan of a place to live and through eating at Happy Hour when, for a dollar drink I could make a meal out of the free h 'oeuvres.

In November a former real estate client asked me to help her sell a mortgage note she owned. Until then I hadn't realized that there was a market for real estate notes. If you own a note and you need money, there are people who will buy the note from you for a discounted price. You get cash now and they get a note that is worth more than they paid, one that pays a higher interest rate then they would get at a bank. Since the note is backed by real estate in case of default, the note holder can foreclose on the property. This is another way to make money from real estate without the expense of buying rentals and the hassle of dealing with tenants.

If I'd known about the note market while I still had money, I probably would have invested. As it was, I earned a commission on the sale of my client's note and sold the notes I held on my former rental property. I can't claim this as a way to make money because I lost money selling my notes at a discount. However, if you have money to invest, you might want to look into the market in buying notes.

89 DOOR TO DOOR SALES

As you might guess, one of the things that suffered during my tenure as a bag lady living in a vacant office building was my self-image. If you will remember, before I leaped off the bureaucratic ship, I thought the worst case scenario would be to lose everything. Well, it seemed that scenario had come to be.

I spent many hours thinking about the choices I made that led me to this sorry state. True, some of them were bad choices, and I had to ask myself what was I thinking?! On the other hand, not everything was my fault. I had no control over Reagan's tax law changes or the savings and loan crisis. In the immortal words of Willie Nelson's song, "Nothing I Can Do About It Now." The only thing left to do was pick myself up and try again.

It never occurred to me that I couldn't get a job. I thought of myself as a very good employee, but no one wanted to hire me. True, I was 45 years old, but I had a degree, was a certified social worker and had a real estate broker's license. With the crash in the economy, my social worker friends were on the street with me and brokers were a dime a dozen.

I couldn't get an entry level job because with my work history they said I would never stay (and they were probably right.) On the other hand, I couldn't get a professional job outside my field because they said I didn't meet the requirements. What a fine kettle of fish! I was either under- or over-qualified for everything.

Totally demoralized, I signed up for a week-long workshop on "How to Have a Good Day." The workshop was conducted by a laid-off social worker who designed the course as her way of surviving the downtime. She reckoned correctly that there were a number of people out there who could benefit from a positive change in attitude.

The workshop consisted of things like counting your blessings while walking in the woods. One thing that sounds bizarre but actually works is to look at yourself in a mirror and repeat, "I'm Happy, I'm

Healthy, I'm Terrific!" (If you emphasize the 'H' and 'T' sounds your diaphragm jumps, releasing serotonin, a mood regulator. Try it, you'll like it!)

By the end of the week, my mood improved dramatically and I decided to put myself in survival mode and wait a year to see if real estate bounced back. If it didn't, I'd go back to school and get into something that would qualify me for a job in the future.

In looking through the want ads, I found a listing for a commission-only job selling a frozen meal package door-to-door. I figured they would hire me because it wouldn't cost them anything. The sales manager was skeptical but agreed to let me try. He gave me a pictorial sales book that explained the product, told how to structure the sales pitch, and gave a price list. The plan consisted of a set of frozen meals that included meats and vegetables. If the mark, I mean prospective buyer, didn't own a freezer, we could sell them one. The company provided leads, the food was good, and a low interest payment plan was available. It seemed like a good deal to me.

The company leads were frequently duds that sent me into places I'd never been before, like Fort Hood and blue-collar neighborhoods. One evening the manager sent me to an upper-class neighborhood. When my knock was answered by a man and woman in Indian dress (from India,) I thought, "Uh oh, this looks like a no-sale to me." However I was not prepared for their reaction.

After we sat down at the dining room table, I propped my sales book up and opened to the first page which pictured sides of beef hanging in a freezer. I will never forget the couple's expressions; they were both horrified. The woman covered her eyes with her hands, jumped up and ran from the room. The man asked me to close the book and explained that they were Hindus, to whom cows were sacred. I apologized and made a hasty retreat.

Over the next six months I sold enough food and freezers to support myself in my reduced circumstances. Eventually I figured out that what we really sold were expensive freezers and that the price per pound for the food was ridiculously high. In good conscience, I could not continue to sell the product. However, the job served its purpose. I got survival money and a job reference that qualified me for entry level positions.

Before I leave this chapter I want to comment on my fellow workers at the frozen meat company. The staff included the supervisor and two young men. The supervisor reminded me of the carnival barkers I encountered at the state fair. One young man was a typical loser type and the other I thought of as a criminal-in-training. He always talked about ways to cheat people and scams to make money. As you can tell, I didn't think much of any of them.

Then one day the headline in the newspaper was about a fire at a local filling station. A gasoline tanker caught on fire in front of the pumps. As the flames leaped higher, it was obvious that the tanker and station were going to blow. The picture that accompanied the article showed the passed-out driver being pulled from the flaming cab to safety by the co-worker I considered a criminal. The article called him a hero. The next time I saw him, he said he was no hero. In fact he said he didn't know why he did it but that someone had to. After that he certainly looked like a hero to me.

90 TEMPS

If you can't get a full-time job or if you need some money but don't want to be tied down to a regular job, a temporary agency might be the right thing for you. Temporary jobs don't pay very much, but they are better than nothing and often lead to offers of full time employment.

On my first visit to a temp agency, I took a typing test. Because I always had a secretary, I hadn't typed in year. The test results certainly reflected my lack of practice: I typed 37 words per minute with an average of 13 mistakes. The office manager suggested I come back when I could type 60 words per minute with no mistakes. I think she thought she would never see me again but she was wrong.

I borrowed a typing book from one of my former secretaries and practiced until I could type well enough to register with the temp agency. The office manager was impressed, not with my typing ability but with my persistence. This lead to a fairly steady if low source of income and a variety of work experiences.

Most were short-term, when a secretary or receptionist was on vacation or sick or when an unusually heavy work load necessitated extra help. I can't even remember where I was or what I did for most of these placements. However, one in particular was memorable. I got a temporary job as secretary for the warden of the Bastrop Federal Correctional Institution.

Bastrop is a minimum security prison where the majority of the inmates are in jail for drug-related offenses. Before sending me to prison, I mean before sending me to the prison, the owner of the temp agency told me that she had an assignment that required some discretion but that she thought I could handle it. I didn't know what to expect as I drove up to the prison gate.

What I didn't expect was a full body search before I passed through the layers of security to get me into the prison but that's what I got. Once inside I was escorted to the warden's office and locked in. I became more and more apprehensive as I sat in the locker room waiting for the warden.

When he finally showed up, he explained that all doors were kept locked to protect staff from the prisoners. (This didn't reduce my apprehension at all.) He took me to the secretary's office, pointed to a mound of paper on the desk and told me his secretary quit about a month ago. He said I would be locked in the secretary's office and that I would need to call for an escort to unlock the door and take me to the restroom (also locked.) He said that we would eat lunch with the prisoners and that he would be back at noon to take me to the cafeteria. He locked the door as he left without telling me what to do. I sat down at the desk and though, "What am I to do now? I can't leave even if I want to."

I sorted the mound of papers into piles of like things and perceived priority. I figured I'd ask the warden to verify the accuracy of the piles and ask for instructions on how to proceed. Although I did not know what most of the items meant, I did recognize one of the papers as a request from a mortgage banker for a character reference. I put that on the top of the pile of things I thought needed the warden's attention.

By lunch time I really, really needed to go to the restroom but the warden had neglected to tell me how to call for an escort. When he retrieved me for lunch I told him I needed to wash my hands and that after lunch I would like some direction. He took me to a restroom labeled "MEN," knocked on the door, and explained as he unlocked the door that they had no ladies' restrooms as there were no women working there except me. It took so long to "wash my hands" that he knocked on the door and asked, "Are you OK?" I was embarrassed, so when I came out of the temporary ladies room, I asked how I was supposed to call for an escort. He looked embarrassed and apologized for neglecting to tell me, but still didn't answer my question.

When we reached the cafeteria what he said about me being the only woman there hit home. The noise level dropped to zero and every eye in the place was on me. We really were eating with the prisoners. As my level of discomfort reached new heights, I involuntarily stepped closer to the warden. He took my arm and led me past the long line of men in prison garb to the front of the line. I walked in lockstep with the warden with my eyes straight ahead.

The food looked like typical institutional fare. After making our selections we joined a table with other prison employees where the warden introduced me as his new secretary. The looks I received made me think they would probably take bets on how long I would last, especially after I tasted the food; if they had let me join the betting pool I'd have bet against myself in a heartbeat. On the way back to my locked office, the warden told me that I didn't have to eat in the cafeteria. I could bring my own lunch or have a tray delivered to my cell—I mean my office.

When the warden unlocked the office, I asked him to come in and comment on my sorted piles. He said he didn't have time but reluctantly stepped through the door. The first thing I handed him was the pile I thought needed his attention. He didn't say anything but visually reacted as he read the request from the mortgage banker. As I wondered what that was all about, he said he would take the rest of that pile with him and would get back to me later on the rest.

Since I was unsure about how to process the remaining piles I decided to look through the files to see what I could learn about the prison. One of the folders contained statistical information. As a federal minimum security facility, 80% of the inmates were incarcerated for drug charges. Only 2% were repeat offenders. The cost per year was shown as $35,000 per prisoner. I was stunned! At that time the welfare payment for a mother and one child in Texas was $87.00 per month x 12 = $1,044.00 per year. We were spending more tax money for guns and guards that we were for children.

As a country, I think we need to take a serious look at our priorities and how the government is spending money. If they legalized marijuana, not only would we empty our prisons and take the drug dealers off the street, but the government would collect enough in taxes to pay off the national debt and pay for clinics to help people get off drugs.

To my relief, by mid-afternoon the warden sent one of the guards to escort me to the unisex restroom. In the late afternoon the warden came to review the piles of paper and answer my questions. Regarding the pile I thought needed his attention he said, "You didn't know it but you saved my bacon by bringing the mortgage broker's letter to my attention." The character reference requested was for his boss.

As I continued the prison job, the work became easier but the routine remained the same. Even though I was given an employee badge, the process to enter the prison stayed the same, and they wouldn't give me a key to either my office or to the restroom.

At the end of the month the warden offered me a permanent job as his secretary, but I declined. Even though the permanent job paid much better than my temp job and I really needed to work, I couldn't reconcile my expectations and the job. I did not believe my destiny was to accept a low-paying dead-end job in a depressing atmosphere.

The warden was obviously disappointed. He asked me to stay until they found someone else and I agreed. The temp agency was also disappointed because the agency would be paid extra money if I took the job, but the manager said she understood. It took the temp agency a month to find someone to take my place and give me a get-out-of-jail-free card.

91 DUPLICATION CLERK

By 1988, real estate had not recovered and I hadn't found a permanent job, so I decided to return to school to prepare myself for a new career, something that would qualify me for jobs in the future. I registered at Austin Community College (ACC) and began working on an associate degree in computer science.

To pay tuition, I learned about Pell Grants. The Federal Pell Grant Program provides need-based grants to low-income students. If you don't have money and want to go to college, I recommend looking into a Pell Grant. Pell Grants are harder to come by now because Congress cut the funding for the program during the last Bush administration and Republicans have blocked subsequent attempts to increase funding and raise the amount. Nevertheless, Pell Grant scholarships help more than 8 million Americans a year afford college.

ACC had a centralized copy room used by all employees. After I registered for college, a friend of mine who worked there got me a job as a duplication clerk. "Duplication Clerk" is a glorified name for someone who stands at the copy machine and makes copies—a totally mindless job, but it paid better than the temp agency and they arranged my schedule so I could take classes. Since I only made copies when someone requested them, the job also provided lots of downtime to study. Another thing the job provided was exposure. I met most of the college employees, or at least their secretaries and teaching assistants. This eventually led to my next job at the college.

92 TEACHING ASSISTANT

By the time I thought my mind was turning to jelly from boredom, I was offered a part time job as an English teaching assistant. The job paid slightly better than the duplication job for fewer hours but was far more interesting. It included a combination of secretarial and teaching tasks for the dean of the English Department. I answered the phone, scheduled appointments and typed, but I also graded tests and counseled students.

Rather than hire full-time professors, ACC hired part-time teachers (now called adjunct faculty) a semester at a time. The stated reason was that the part-timers had knowledge of current business practices. However, the real reason was that this practice saved the college major money as full-time professors were paid a starting salary of $40,000 a year with benefits, while part-timers were paid about $2,000 a semester per class with no benefits. Also, the educational requirements were not the same and it was easy to get rid of unsatisfactory teachers. They could be dismissed by simply not renewing their contract.

When the dean got to know me, he turned the responsibility of interviewing, screening and scheduling prospective teachers over to me. He interviewed and approved my selections. This worked out well because both of us could deny responsibility if the people who were not hired came to complain. They would have to come to me to schedule an appointment with the dean. I would sympathize with them and tell them about the limited number of positions and the unlimited number of applicants, and would explain that I had no control over who was hired. If they still wanted to see the dean, he would tell them that he had no control over the screening process and could only interview the applicants who were referred to him.

If a teacher couldn't make a class, I helped find a substitute. Since I had the minimum requirements to substitute in a pinch, I became the substitute teacher. Also, as I learned programming, I automated the office. This was a wonderful job that made me realize what a great life academia provides. In fact I enjoyed it so much I was sorry to leave. If it paid more I might have stayed and my story would end here.

93 TAX EXAMINER

While going to school and working as a teaching assistant I was still looking for a job either in real estate or social work. Reagan's tax law changes had a far reaching effect on the investment value of property. I had attended a couple of workshops on the subject but was still trying to understand the impact when I saw an ad for a seasonal job at the IRS. I decided to apply for the job because I thought it would help me understand the changes and I could still go to school and keep my part-time college job by working the night shift.

In 1988, at age 46, I got a seasonal job as a Grade 4 tax examiner at the Austin Service Center. The job paid $13,513 a year plus benefits, which was more than I'd made since the real estate crash in 1985. Benefits included health insurance, life insurance, a retirement pension, Social Security, and a 401K plan.

Although I was pleased with the job offer, I felt there was some kind of karma involved. As a realtor, I had been audited several times by IRS. I always paid my taxes and there was never a problem, but the process was always unpleasant. One time an auditor gave me a particularly hard time. As I left the office I thought, "Who would work there! If no one would work there they would have to go out of business!" Well, I found out who would work there—me.

When I got the job at IRS, my work day started at 7:00 a.m. I took classes from 7:00 a.m. to 11:00 a.m., worked at the college from 11:00 a.m. to 3:00 p.m., and then worked as a tax examiner for the IRS from 4:00 p.m. to 1:00 a.m. You might notice that this schedule left precious little time for eating, sleeping and study. In retrospect I wonder how I did it but at the time, I just figured you do what you have to do.

Until the oil, banking and real estate crash in Texas, seasonal jobs at IRS were perfect for blue-collar house wives. On the night shift, women didn't have to pay child care because the kids could be left at home with their dad. Most jobs lasted six to eight months and laid-off employees could keep their insurance; they qualified for unemployment until called back to work for the next tax season. Work time counted towards time-in-grade pay raises and toward qualifying for a federal pension. After the crash, more and more of the seasonal jobs went to former bankers, builders, realtors, real estate attorneys, appraisers, and mortgage loan officers. The cars in the parking lot went from old pickup trucks to Cadillacs, Lincoln Town Cars, and Mercedes Benzes. All of us former high rollers were delighted to get the jobs.

At that time all tax returns were submitted on paper and processed in service centers around the country. The work of processing returns was divided into functions collectively called The Pipeline. The Pipeline was organized like a factory line, where returns were passed from function to function until processing was complete. Pipeline employees were "measured" based on how many transactions they completed. Seasonal employee were released (laid off) and recalled (rehired) based on transactions processed.

My first job was working the night shift in an error correction section called Unpostables. Returns that did not match a record on the master file were returned for research and correction. My section was located upstairs in a back corner about as far from the front door as you could get. We were given 30 minutes to eat dinner and two 15 minute breaks. After three weeks on the floor counting transactions, I realized that the way to go was to get an "unmeasured" position.

Fortunately for me, the Branch Chief asked for a volunteer who knew something about computers. I quickly raised my hand. Three weeks later, I was promoted to a Grade 5 tax examiner making $15,118 a year, moved from the night shift to the day shift and from the back of the building to the front as the Automation Coordinator for the Processing Division Chief. I happily quit my day job and signed up for night classes.

Before I left the floor, my night manager told me about an OPM test for the position of computer programmer trainee. If I passed the test and the interview, I would be hired and the government would provide training for me to become a computer programmer. Since I was already working on an associate degree in computer science, this seemed like an ideal program for me. In 1988 I took the test and was interviewed but never heard the results. I assumed I didn't get the job.

I really enjoyed working in the Processing Division office. The division chief wanted some customized reports extracted from a national report called the Work Planning & Control Report (WP & C for short.) This report, produced in Washington, D.C., was based on data from all IRS Service Centers. The report, printed each week, was 927 pages long. To analyze the data, information from the report was typed into PC's. If updates to the national report were needed, a key punch machine was used to input data.

Because of my community college classes, I knew that data could be transferred from the mainframe computer directly to PC's, then transferred back to the mainframe. This would eliminate the need to input data, saving hundreds of staff hours. However, in 1988 the Austin Service center owned only five PC's and none of them had hard drives to store data. I solved this problem by adding hard drives to the PC's, and then wrote a program to transfer the data from the mainframe to the PC's. This allowed me to produce the reports the director wanted.

At the end of the tax season I was offered a full time job as a Grade 6 automation coordinator making $16,851 a year. You might think that I would jump at the job but you would be wrong. Considering my prior circumstances and qualifications, I couldn't imagine that $16,851 a year was the best that I could do.

When I declined the job offer, I was laid off and did not expect to return to IRS. Later events would prove me wrong. Over the next couple of years I continued to work on my associate degree in computer science and continued to look for career opportunities. I worked two more tax seasons, 1989 and 1990, for the IRS in Austin before that opportunity came along.

94 OPPORTUNITY KNOCKS

In 1988, my mother was diagnosed with colon cancer and expected the worst, so I made arrangements to move to Fort Worth, Texas, to take care of her. However, by the time I actually moved, the cancerous growth had been removed and she did not need anyone to take care of her. Her version of my move was that I was unemployed and had returned home for her to take care of me. Things went downhill from there.

The job market in Fort Worth was worse than Austin, and without my Austin network of friends, I had no one to help me find work. Fortunately for me, an Austin acquaintance asked me to go to Hawaii with her for three weeks in December. She was a travel agent with free first- class airfare and hotels, but no money to pay for other things. She said, "I have been looking for Prince Charming to go with me but haven't found him yet. If you can pay for a rental car and food, you can go with me and I'll continue my search there."

When she called, I didn't have the money but what I did have was a 1959 Pontiac that I used as a touring car when I sold real estate. Since I no longer had a home or office, I had no place to park the behemoth and had left it with a friend. I agreed to go with her and made arrangements to sell the Pontiac at a car auction.

My mother and sister both thought I was nuts. They thought I should stay home and look for work. I balanced a free trip to Hawaii against a futile search for work and voted to go. The trip was incredible in many ways but that's a story for another time.

When I returned from Hawaii, the Austin IRS called me back to work as a seasonal employee. However with no money and no place to live, the trick was to figure out how to get back to Austin. Fortunately my network of friends came through again. A friend who spent most of his time at his girlfriend's house offered to rent me a room, since several years before I rented a room to him when he needed a place. I had the full run of the house except for a storage shed he kept locked. Essentially I was there alone pet sitting for his two cats; my dog soon joined the cats as the friend who was keeping her could no longer do so.

I felt quite comfortable at his house partly because he had taken a number of my prize possessions to his house on long-term temporary loan and many of the things he had, such as his toaster and hammock, were identical to things I used to have. However, when I commented on the similarity, I thought his reaction was strange. He denied the similarity and obviously didn't want to talk about it.

Since the seasonal job was at night, I re-enrolled at Austin Community College to continue my quest for an associate degree in computer science. Things moved along smoothly until September of 1989, when my friend announced that he was being transferred to Daytona Beach, Florida, and I would have to move. I didn't have enough money saved to pay deposits on an apartment, so he offered to pay me to paint his house to get it ready for sale. We agreed that after the movers took his things, I would camp out in the house for a month while I painted all the rooms. So I guess I can add "house painter" to the list of ways I have tried to make money.

I helped him pack up his house and on the day the movers came, I helped him pack his car. As Dick and the movers prepared to leave, I ran out to tell him that he forgot to pack the storage shed. He told me that he had not forgotten and that I could have anything in the shed I wanted. After they left, I opened the door to the shed and was dumbfounded. The shed contained all the leftovers from the garage sale I had when I moved out of my house, including the things like the toaster and hammock I recognize in the house. These were the things that were supposed to go to the Salvation Army! As I stood there in shock I remembered that my friend had been one of the last people to come to my garage sale. He asked me what I planned to do with the stuff that was left over. I told him it was to go to the Salvation Army. He asked "Can I have anything I want?" I said, "Sure." Thus the mystery of what happened to the leftovers in my garage was solved. I called the Salvation Army to come get the stuff I promised them two years earlier.

When I finished painting the house in October I found a duplex I could afford to rent and moved my stuff out of the condo garage. The house looked pretty bare until my friends heard that I had rented a place. I had not asked them to return the things they had taken home on long-term temporary loan because I didn't know how stable my situation was. However, one by one almost everything came back to me. I could count on one hand the things that never made it home.

Shortly after moving in, I was laid off from my seasonal Job with the IRS. They told me they did not expect to need an Unpostable section for the next filing season, so I probably would not be called back to work. I had enough money to last until the first of February, 1990.

By January first, my unemployment benefits had ended and I had had no luck in finding work. Since I was going to school, I could not sign up with one of the temporary agencies. The only money I had was $50.00 I received as a Christmas present and $200.00 my mother gave me to replace a contact lens I lost. I used the $50.00 to buy food and had no idea how I would pay the rent for February. Things had really bottomed out.

On Sunday, January 7, a friend invited me to go to the Unity Church with her. The church had a new female pastor that I had heard good things about, so I was happy to go. The service was very good. At the end, the pastor announced that a prosperity seminar was scheduled for that afternoon and we were all invited to attend. Since I was definitely in need of some prosperity, I decided to attend.

The principal speaker was Edwene Gaines, a leading prosperity teacher. According to her bio, she overcame poverty to live a lifestyle of wealth by following *The Four Spiritual Laws of Prosperity*, the title of her latest book. She talked about finding your divine purpose, forgiveness and worthiness, tithing, and giving and setting clear-cut goals. She told us to write down on a piece of paper three things we wanted. I listed an immediate job and a career. I thought if I had those two things, I could get anything else I wanted, but since she said three things, I added a new car to the list. My existing car had over 100,000 miles on it and needed work I could not afford.

At the end of the seminar she re-emphasized the importance of tithing 10%. As I said earlier, the only money I had was the $200.00 my mother sent to replace my contacts. I thought, "You know, it can't get much worse than this" so I gave her $20.00.

As we left the building Edwene passed out prosperity cards that read: "This has been blessed with prosperity for you. Make this statement daily: The Inexhaustible Resource of Spirit is equal to every demand. There is no reality in lack. Abundance is here and now manifests."

The seminar was on Sunday. Monday I received a call from the IRS in Austin asking me to return to work immediately. Since the IRS paid every two weeks, that meant I would receive a pay check in time to pay my rent. I thought, "Thank you, Dear God, for my job!"

Tuesday I received a call from the IRS in Washington, D.C. Remember the test I took in 1988 for the Computer Programmer Training Program? They wanted to know if I was still interested. When I said yes, they told me they would pay for me to come to Washington for a three-month training class. At the end of the class I would be offered a Grade 7 career ladder job with automatic promotions to Grade 12. They would also pay relocation expenses. I thought, "Thank you, Dear God, for my career!"

Wednesday, as I was backing out of my driveway, I heard a loud popping sound and smoke started pouring out of the engine. I started to panic, but then remembered that I had put a new car on the list of things I wanted. I knew that as long as my car ran I would not do anything to get a new car. I decided this was God's way of making sure I got a new car, so I drove my smoking car two blocks to a used car lot where I sold it for $300.00. I then went to Enterprise Car Rentals and rented a car. As I drove out of the lot, I affirmed that I would somehow get the money to buy a new car before the rental car had to be returned.

Thursday I received a call from a friend. Her parents were in town and wanted to buy a house for cash with a quick closing; she wanted to know if I would help them. Friday, I received another call asking me to help a friend buy a tract of land for cash. In ten years in real estate, I had handled only one cash transaction. Of course I said yes to both. Both transactions closed in three weeks and I made $8,500.00.

I had the rental car for a month. With a week left, I looked for a car that I could buy with the money I had. My only criterion was that the car needed to be a late model and of a type that had a good track record for not needing repairs. All the dealers I approached wanted me to use the $8,500.00 as a down payment and finance the rest. Since my financial future was uncertain, I was totally unwilling to take on a car payment. Someone suggested that I talk to the car rental places as they sold their used cars with new warranties. I called Hertz and said, "I have $8,500.00 to buy a car. What can you sell me?" The salesman told me that he had a 1989 white Toyota Corolla and a blue one that he could probable sell for that price. I told him that I was on my way.

When I arrived at Hertz, the salesman on the floor was not the one I talked to on the phone. He told me that he did not know why the other salesman told me I could buy the Corolla for $8,500.00. He said the blue one was already sold and the white one was listed at $12,500.00. He said he would talk to his manager but he didn't think the deal would go. He offered to take my money as down payment and finance the rest. Since this was the same song and dance I received from all the dealers, I told him to talk to the manager and have him call me if he wanted to sell the car. I left thinking I'd never hear from him.

Much to my surprise the Hertz manager called me the following Thursday. . He asked if I really had cash and if I could close by Friday. When I said, "Yes," he said, "I would not normally do this but I need the sale to make my quota for this month. If you can close by tomorrow, I'll sell you the white corolla for $8,500.00." I said, "I'm on my way."

I arrived at the dealer's with certified check in hand and was ushered into the office to complete the paperwork. As soon as we sat down, the salesman started talking about tax, title, license, delivery charges and extended warranty. When he finished his list of additional charges, I held up my check for $8,500.00 and shook my head no, saying, "I'm sorry, this is all I have." He told me I had to pay the extra charges or he couldn't sell me the car. I repeated, "I'm sorry, but this really is all I have, so I guess we can't make a deal." As I stood up to go, he gave me a look of total shock. When he realized that I really intended to walk out, his look turned to alarm. He said, "Wait! Let me talk to the manager."

After a long wait the manager came into the room where I was sitting. He told me that the fees really had to be paid. I said, "I know, but $8,500.00 really is all the money I have." I explained that I had been unemployed until a couple of weeks ago and that my first pay check would only cover the rent. I said if I needed to pay more than the $8500.00, I could not buy the car. When the manager didn't say anything, I thanked him for his time, stood up and walked towards the dealership door, thinking that I would have to use some of the purchase money to continue the car lease. As I reached to open the door, the manager said, "Wait! You can have the car." He looked so unhappy about selling me the car that I tried to suppress my excitement and joy. I thought "Thank you, Dear God, for my car!"

In one month I had gone from no money, no job, no prospects, and no way to pay my rent to a job, a career, and a new car all as a result of an afternoon prosperity seminar. I became a believer in affirmations. To this day I keep the prosperity card on my dresser and read it daily. (I know some of you are skeptical and I don't blame you. I was once a skeptic too. However I have no other explanation for the series of events described above or for some subsequent things that happened.)

95 PROGRAMMER

Since I was hired as an IRS seasonal employee in Austin, without consulting me, my manager asked the IRS National Office in Washington to postpone my training until the end of tax season. They agreed and scheduled me for a training class that started in August, 1999.

Initially I was not happy with the postponement but on reflection I realized the delay would allow me time to complete my associate degree in computer science and to accumulate some money. In addition, the English Department at Austin Community College called and offered to let me return to my teaching assistant job; the person they hired to replace me had quit. This meant once again my schedule would run from 7:00 a.m. to 12:00 a.m. an 18-hour workday, but that was OK. I really loved working at the college.

Time passed quickly and August soon arrived. Between my two jobs, I managed to save $5,000.00. I made arrangements for a friend to stay in my duplex to take care of my dog and for another friend to take over my ACC job with the understanding that she would give it back if I returned. That way, if the Washington job didn't work out, I would still have a place to live and a job. With my fallback position assured, I headed off to Washington, D.C. for the training to become a computer programmer for the federal government.

When I arrived in Washington in August, 1990, my first question was why it took three years to hire me since I took the test for the program in 1988. The explanation was that there was a hiring freeze from 1988 to 1990 which meant they couldn't hire anyone. When the freeze was lifted they called me.

When the class started, I was somewhat disconcerted to discover that what they were teaching was an obsolete version of COBOL. I knew it was obsolete because I had studied the current version at ACC. When I asked why they were teaching an older version they explained that all the IRS computers were old, with programs written in obsolete ALC or COBOL. The basic computer programing classes were necessary because the obsolete languages were no longer taught in schools and programmers who knew them did not want to use them.

After the first test, I learned that, out of a class of 30, only three of us had any background in computers. The other two were programmers who signed up for the class as a way to get a federal job. Almost all the other people were what I thought of as "upwardly mobile secretaries or tax examiners." That is, they were already federal employees who applied for the class because of the career ladder (automatic promotions from pay grades 5, 7, 9, 11 to Grade 12.)

After the third test, the three of us who had programming backgrounds were so far ahead of the rest of the class that management offered to let us drop out of the program and be hired as Grade 12 employees. The other two quickly accepted the offer. In retrospect, I should have accepted also. However the problem was relocation.

Through the training program, the government would pay for the move and provide a housing allowance for up to a year. For a direct hire, they could do neither. When I explained my concern, they told me that if I stayed with the program I would be hired as a Grade 7 employee. Then, at the end of the first year, I could quit my Grade 7 job and be rehired as a Grade 12. I opted to stay with the program.

At the end of the class, I was officially hired as a Grade 7 programmer with a relocation housing allowance of $1,400. This allowed me to rent the second floor of a wonderfully-furnished Georgetown mansion with a crystal chandelier, fireplace, oriental carpets, a patio deck and antique furniture. Upon delivery, my own stuff went into storage. I could happily have stayed there forever except for the fact that when the housing allowance ended, my take home pay was not enough to pay the rent, much less groceries and dog food. I began my quixotic search for a permanent home in Georgetown that I could rent for less than $1,000 a month.

A search of rental prices re-affirmed how quixotic the search really was, as normal rentals for a one-bedroom apartment in Georgetown ran from $2,000 to $3,000 a month. I reasoned that the real deals would not be listed in the newspaper, but would be found by word of mouth, so I expanded my search by taking my dog to Montrose Park to meet the neighbors. My first lead was to an English basement apartment on Q Street, NW. The apartment had 1500 square feet and a back yard and would have been ideal for me and my dog except for the fact that the place was a dump and the landlord wanted $900 a month. Oh, well, my search continued.

The relocation money was running out and I began to think I would never find a permanent home in Georgetown. I broadened my search to include roommate situations (grim) and housing outside Georgetown. When I looked into the real estate rental market outside Georgetown, I was dismayed to find out that my new job, salary, credit history, dog, and piano were all liabilities that made me a persona non grata to the real estate agents; finding any home in a desirable location was going to be more difficult than I thought. I was starting to despair when my luck changed.

The neighbor who originally told me about the $900 apartment mentioned that the place was still vacant and that the owner's car had broken down. Previously I had told her my miracle story about my new car. She suggested that I might be able to work something out with him if I let him use my car. I remembered the condition of the apartment but reasoned I could clean it and fix it.

When I approached the owner, my first surprise was that the apartment had been cleaned and painted by a Hungarian immigrant who worked for a contractor that lived in the neighborhood. The man was doing the work in exchange for a place to stay while he worked. He was camping out there with only a bed, a chair, and a television.

Since I was hired on a 7-9-11-12 career ladder, my income would increase each year for three years. The deal I offered the owner was a three-year contract for $650 rent the first year, $750 the second and $850 the third, plus he could use my car for two years. He accepted the offer and told me the rent also included utilities and cable. I was ecstatic! With little income, bad credit and a dog, I had landed the perfect apartment for me on Q Street NW in the heart of Georgetown.

Bob Woodward, the Washington Post writer who broke the Watergate story, lived across the street, the Italian ambassador lived next door and Donna Shalala, the Secretary of Health and Human Services under President Bill Clinton, lived around the corner.

The next hurdle was to get my stuff out of long-term storage where it had languished for almost a year. When I called the company, they told me the storage contract was for a year and they would not deliver my things until the end of the contract. What to do? Now I had my dream apartment but nothing to put in it.

Not to worry: the Hungarian workman offered to lend me the bed and chair he was using, but not the television. When I went to Blockbusters to see if I could rent a television, the kid working there told me they did not rent televisions and he did not know anyone who did. However he had a television his parents gave him that I could have. As he helped me load the television into my car, I asked him if he wanted it back when my own television was delivered. He told me no, that I should pass it on to someone else who needed it.

I moved out of my temporary Georgetown mansion into my new empty home. As I sat in my borrowed chair with my dog on my lap, watching my gift television sitting on a cardboard box, I couldn't help but marvel at, and be thankful for, the perseverance and miracles that brought me to this place.

Back on the job front, after I finished the obsolete COBOL class I was assigned to a section that used UNIX, C, and SQL with an ORACLE data base - all state of the art programming languages in 1990. To illustrate the difference, the printout of the code for the old COBOL program we wrote in class was three inches thick. Just for practice, I rewrote the program in C. The printout was one page.

My section was created to take over a system called the Total Employee Performance System (TEPS) written by contractors. The set of programs was used to release and recall seasonal employees. In a karmic loop these programs used the same Work Plan and Control Data that I had worked with my first season with IRS. The programs ran as stand-alone systems in the ten IRS Service Centers and nothing worked right. At first, my job consisted of providing help desk support to the beleaguered data base administrators in the service centers and emergency repairs when the programs crashed. The programs took about five hours to run and the National Treasury Employees Union filed a national grievance challenging the results. I analyzed the code and proposed a redesign to solve the problems. The proposal was accepted by the Union and management. The redesign reduced runtime from five hours to five minutes and resolved the grievance.

I mention the TEPS work because the job and the redesign required massive amounts of overtime, a welcome supplement to my meager salary. At the time overtime pay was capped at the grade 10 level, which meant you did not receive time-and-a-half based on your regular salary. Because of this, some people refused to work overtime. I'd spent so many years working overtime for no pay that it didn't matter to me. It was still money I wouldn't have otherwise.

Also, during my first year as a permanent federal employee I discovered some other things that increased my income: yearly cost-of-living adjustments (COLA) and the fact that the government matched the first 5% of money employees add to their Thrift Savings Plan (TSP = 401K.) If you didn't save money, you didn't get the match. I couldn't afford to save 5 % of my salary that first year but I realized I could reach that goal by increasing my savings by the amount of the COLA each year until I reached 5%. After all, the COLA represented money I didn't have so I wouldn't miss it. In later years I met employees who said they couldn't afford to add money to the TSP. I thought they couldn't afford not to.

My office was at 12th Street and Pennsylvania Avenue in downtown Washington. Called "America's Main Street," Pennsylvania Avenue is the street that joins the White House and the United States Capitol. I had a great boss, liked my co-workers, and enjoyed my job. Everything was coming up roses until the end of the year when I was to quit my Grade 7 job and be rehired as a Grade 12 programmer.

A job fair was scheduled. To make sure there were no problems, my boss volunteered to be the interviewer at the fair and made arrangements with Personnel to handle the paperwork. He helped me prepare my application and everything was set.

Unfortunately, the job fair was cancelled and a hiring freeze went into effect that lasted until after I reached Grade 12 on my career ladder, three years down the road. Because of grade and step increases, the 1990 decision to stay with the training program Grade 7 job instead of taking the Grade 12 job offer cost me more than $66,000 in lost wages.

In retrospect, it seems as though I made a bad decision. However, if I'd taken the Grade 12 job I would not have ended up in my bargain Georgetown apartment that saved me over $222,000 in rent and utilities over my 10-year stay. Who can really know the impact of the road not taken? As a footnote, during that time I did manage to pay off the $25,000 debt I incurred in 1986 and 1987 trying to keep my Austin house from foreclosure.

All told, I worked for the IRS for 23 years. The stories of my time spent there would turn this collection of short stories into a novel. Although I know of a former IRS employee who received a $400,000 advance for writing an exposé of the internal workings of the agency, it is not my intention at this time to write an exposé. Since this collection is about my attempts to make money, I'll focus on the decisions I made to increase my wealth.

96 TAX SYSTEMS MODERNIZATION/ANALYST

By the time I was eligible for a promotion to a Grade 13 position, I learned that at the time there was no career path for programmers beyond Grade 12. If I wanted to go any higher, I would have to go into management or change career paths. I had no desire to be a manager with the IRS, so I decided to look for another career path. My first opportunity came when they were looking for volunteers to work on tax system modernization (TSM.) I volunteered and received a temporary promotion to Grade 13. This also led to more overtime pay. TSM was a massive effort to upgrade the computer systems to bring the IRS into the 20th century. Part of the plan was a contract with IBM to develop a system to image tax returns and store data. I was assigned to develop a proposal for a transition bridge that would link the data in the new system to the older systems that were not included in the planned upgrade. My proposal was accepted and I was assigned to design and program the transition bridge. As it turned out, my piece of the system was the only part that worked.

At that time TSM was the largest information technology reform ever undertaken by a U.S. civilian agency. Work continued from 1990 to 1996 before the modernization effort was halted by Congress. On January 31, 1997, the New York Times News Service ran a story with the headline: "IRS admits its $4 billion modernizing is a failure." and a sub-head "Official says computers don't work; agency wants to contract out tax returns." The article stated that the IRS conceded that their modern computer systems "do not work in the real world..." On a personal front, this meant I lost my temporary promotion and returned to my former Grade 12 salary.

97 CONFIGURATION MANAGEMENT

Next I applied for a configuration management position with IRS that was not included in the in-house listings because the director of that section stated that no one in house had the qualifications for the job. I did. "Configuration management" is the collective name for a set of processes used to identify computer hardware and software and to track and control changes. My training in configuration management went all the way back to the time when I worked on the design, development and implementation of the computerized welfare system for the State of Texas. In fact, when I came to work for the IRS, I was amazed that there was no configuration management system in place. I was one of two in-house employees hired with a promotion to Grade 13. I got the promotion but my section refused to release me. I didn't know they could do that but it seems they could.

A few months later there was a reorganization that moved the Configuration Management section to a new division. The new division director was a crusty old lady who swore like a sailor. She came to my desk and wanted to know why in the H#!! I had not reported to my new job. I explained that my section refused to release me. She said: "We'll see about that! You belong to me. Get your stuff and come now!" I piled my stuff up on my desk chair and wheeled it down the hall to my new office. My old boss was not a happy camper, but there was nothing he could do about it since I was now in a different division.

When I reported to the Configuration Management section chief who hired me, he told me that the new division director was crazy and said: "I'm leaving and I suggest you get out of here as soon as you can!" What a wonderful way to start a new job!

I soon learned that his assessment was correct and started my search for a new place to work. I had three immediate job offers but now my new section chief refused to release me. Since none of the offers involved a promotion, there was nothing I could do but look for a new job with a promotion to Grade 14. Before that happened the division director was replaced and a reorganization eliminated the division. We were all transferred with the director back to the IT organization in the division that tested computer systems.

98 STRATEGIC PLANNING

My opportunity for a promotion to Grade 14 came when the IRS started a new modernization effort called Business Systems Modernization (BSM). Once again I volunteered and received a temporary Grade 14. This time Booz Allen Hamilton, a contracting firm, was hired to work with the IRS to develop plans and processes for modernizing the IT organization. I was assigned to develop a proposal for a strategic planning process. The proposal I developed was accepted and a strategic planning section was created in the Finance Division. At the end of the project I went to work in the newly created section with a permanent Grade 14.

A few years down the road, my time as a strategic planner ended when everyone in my division was called into a meeting. We were told that a reorganization was planned and our division was being eliminated. All the managers were going to other positions and employees who could not find another job would be laid off. This is not exactly the news you want to hear when you are approaching retirement age.

My manager had accepted a job in the Small Business section of the IRS (SB/SE), so I asked her if she could help me find a job there too. She told me about a vacancy in the SB/SE Planning Division. I applied and got the job. I later learned that the IT organization did not plan to eliminate the Strategic Planning Section I was in, but instead planned to transfer it to another division. However, since they did not tell us in time, everyone in the section found other jobs.

99 EMPLOYEE SATISFACTION

One of the functions included in the SB/SE Planning Division was employee satisfaction. This program was mandated by Congress with the Internal Revenue Service Restructuring and Reform Act of 1998 (RRA '98.) Among other things RRA'98 included provisions to assess organizational performance on equally weighted measures of business results, customer satisfaction, and employee satisfaction. The IRS contracted with survey companies to conduct employee and customer satisfaction surveys. Each functional area had survey program managers to manage the surveys within their function and to see that action was taken on survey results.

Not too long after I came to work for SB/SE, responsibility for the SB/SE employee satisfaction survey was transferred from Planning to Personnel (Human Resources.) Another employee and I were transferred with the program. Before I became an Employee Satisfaction Program Manager for SB/SE, I'd always considered employee satisfaction in the IRS to be somewhat of an oxymoron. Although I very much enjoyed my tenure with the program and working with my co-workers, the experience did not alter my opinion. In fact before the survey was discontinued, the IRS changed the name from Employee Satisfaction to Employee Engagement. Most employees viewed this name change as a shift in management priorities from "What can we do for you?" to "What can you do for us?"

This job did not bring a change in salary, but it did bring the opportunity to work at home. There were 40 employees scattered across the country who were assigned to work with me as a collateral duty. This meant they reported to my co-worker and me on matters related to employee satisfaction but we were not responsible for personnel issues—the best of both worlds in my opinion. Except for occasional conferences and meetings, almost everything we did was on the phone or on the computer, so there was no reason to go into the office.

Until I started working at home, I didn't realize the cost of work, that is, how much money I spent to work in an office. First, there were the obvious costs for the commute, lunches, and coffee breaks. With a 50-mile a day commute, eating out for lunch, and a Starbucks in the building I was shocked to discover I spent about $600 a month on those three things alone. Then there were the less obvious costs for things like make-up, accessories, dry cleaning, work clothes, and general running-around money. If you ever have the opportunity to work at home, jump on it and save the savings.

100 PRE-RETIREMENT

At long last, I'm almost to the end of this story but I still have a few gaps to fill in and some more things to say about how I made money. If you will remember, one way to improve your bottom line is to reduce your expenses. In 1990 I already had one of the best deals in the world in my Georgetown rent of $875 a month, utilities included. However, in 1994 a friend moved in with me and my share of the rent dropped to $437.50 a month. (Note: Get a roommate.)

In 1996, my mother passed away. She was not wealthy but had been comfortably well off. My sisters and I shared the inheritance which was enough to pay the down payment on a house with money left over for remodeling. (Note: Inherit if you can)

In 1997, my office moved from downtown D.C. to New Carrollton, Maryland, half-way between Annapolis, Maryland, and Washington. My commute to work from Georgetown took me through some of the roughest neighborhoods in D.C. at a time when D.C. was considered the murder capital of the world. I began to think about buying a home (Note: Buy a house.)

In 1998 my Georgetown landlord announced that he planned to sell his house for $475,000. As his tenant I had first right of refusal. Left to my own devices, I would have bought the place. It was in bad shape, but it sat on a block with properties worth two to three million. Remodeled and restored it would be in the one to two million range at least. Because of my real estate experience, I knew I could rent the apartment for enough to pay the mortgage, leaving money free to pay for the badly-needed remodeling. However, my significant other did not understand how we could afford to buy and remodel the place. (Note: Recognize and act on a good deal when it is offered.)

I turned on the computer and began research to find us a new home. My search was aided by the fact that property values were depressed and interest rates were low. Since my office was now closer to Annapolis, Maryland than to Georgetown, I decided to research property in Annapolis as well as in D.C. For Annapolis, my only criteria was water access or a water view and a garage. Everyone told me that Annapolis was too expensive and that I would never find property near water that I could afford.

The first thing I did was make a list of properties in our price range that appealed to me for one reason or another. Once I had my list, I grouped the properties by location and researched sold properties in those areas to determine average market value. I reasoned that if there were several properties in one area that appealed to me, that increased the likelihood of finding something I wanted in that area. Knowing the average market value would help me recognize bargains and help negotiate the best price. For example, one of the properties on my list was described as being waterfront but was listed at lot value for the area. Without seeing the house, I knew it must be a tear-down or in need of remodeling. List in hand, I made an appointment with a realtor. (Note: Know what you want.)

When we pulled in to the driveway of the 900-square foot house listed as "waterfront," my first thought was, "Ugh! My dream house does not have vinyl siding and asbestos shingles." It was built as a beach house in the '50s and occupied by tenants since the '70s. It really was a dump. My fiancé whispered, "Why are we looking at this place?"

Walking into the living room we both knew why. The house is waterfront, across from Gibson Island, where the Magothy River enters the Chesapeake Bay. The view is spectacular with one and a half miles of water to Gibson Island, four miles to the opposite bank, the Chesapeake to the right and Deep Creek River to the left. As we stood there in awe, my fiancé said, "Only restaurants have this kind of view!" After seeing the water, his mind was made up. His enthusiasm was so obvious that the realtor knew the house was sold. I wasn't so sure. I had a clear image of what I wanted to do with the house but it needed so much work! I wanted to be sure that we didn't put more money into the house than it was worth. Remember, I had a house underwater once and did not want to repeat that experience! (Note: Have a clear image of the result you want.)

When we got home, I drew a picture of the house as I saw it in my mind and started estimating how much it would cost to turn the sow's ear that existed into the silk purse I imagined. Every house I had remodeled had something to save, like hardwood floors or a stone exterior, but not this one. The best way would be to tear it down and build a new house on the lot. However, we did not have that luxury. Because the house was within 100 feet of the water getting a permit to build would be time-consuming and we needed an immediate place to live. The solution was to build around the core of the house. Following is the sanitized version of how I accomplished the remodeling. I say "sanitized" because the whole story would take a book titled The Remodel from Hell. In this one I'm just going to cover the highlights dealing with money.

Since the sales price of the house was really just the value of the lot, I finished the rough estimate and the numbers worked. The remodeled house would be worth more than the mortgage. We bought the house in December, 1998, for $235,000 and moved in February, 1999. I developed a strategic plan for the remodeling and a plan to get the necessary money. Since we were buying the house for the water view, I started on the water side, using the money I had inherited from my mother. Once that was done, the value of the house increased, and I took out a second mortgage to get the money to do the street side. In other words the house itself provided the money for the second phase of the remodeling.

The work took an upscale tick when my neighbor, who was also remodeling her house, took me to a builder's auction house called Southern Sales and Service. I wanted a cherry kitchen but had decided the price was too high. When we walked in the building, there was my cherry kitchen! There were forty feet of cherry kitchen cabinets lined against the wall - the same cabinets I had originally priced. Even the knobs were what I wanted! The auctioneer told me the cabinets came out of a model home. When I won the bid for $5,000, the seller informed me that the cabinets also came with Corian countertops and all the appliances. Later, as we were loading the cabinets into a truck, he said: "That's a $65,000 kitchen."

As I was contemplating a dream come true, my husband was freaking out, wanting to know where we were going to put the cabinets until we were ready to install them. Fortunately the house had an unfinished basement where the cabinets could stay while I worked out the plan for the kitchen.

As it turned out, I ended up with a cherry kitchen, cherry bathroom and utility room. I also bought Anderson windows, travertine floors, a granite bathroom, doors and fixtures from the auction house. When all was said and done, I refinanced the house to pay off the second mortgage and the house appraised for $1,300,000.00. I was shocked! This was the first time I didn't want a high appraisal because it would raise our taxes. We had our mini mansion set up for our retirement home. (Note: Buy a home you can afford. Remodel if you can do so within market.)

In 2007 I became eligible for Social Security. Even though I was still working, I decided to apply because I wanted to maximize the money in my 401K and pay off bills. My goal was to be debt-free by the time I retired. My husband did the same thing. (Note: Pay off debt and save as much as you can.)

When interest rates dropped, I refinanced the house, not to draw out money but to lower the mortgage. (Note: Reduce bills as much as possible.)

Originally we planned to retire in 2008. Our financial advisor told us we would have enough money to last us into our nineties. Then the stock market crashed. At first he told us we still had enough to carry us into our eighties. Then we lost enough that we had money to last only into our seventies. He said, "You might want to keep your job. Remembering what happened to me in the '80s, I started to hyperventilate. My internal voice said, "Wait! This time you have a job and a husband." At age 66, 70 was not that far off so I decided to take his advice.

With the crash of the stock market, real estate also took a nose dive and the value of our house fell. The next time interest rates dropped and I had the house appraised for refinancing, the value had dropped from $1,300,000 to $700,000. But since we didn't plan to sell, that was OK with me. A lower value translates into lower taxes and therefore a lower mortgage payment.

(There are a couple of notes here. First, hire a good financial planner to help you get your affairs in order. Following his advice, I saved more than enough to pay his bill. Next, the future is guaranteed to no one. Even if you do everything you're "supposed" to do, thing happen. Learn to deal with what is.)

101 RETIRED

By 2010 the stock market had recovered enough that at least on paper we had enough resources to retire. At first I was skeptical (read "afraid.") By then we were both eligible for federal retirement pensions and Social Security and we both had 401K plans and Thrift Savings, Medicare and Blue Cross Blue Shield, life insurance and long term care insurance. We had our wonderful waterfront house with affordable payments and equity and no other debt. We were paid for unused vacation time, so we also had a pot of money to pay for a bucket list of trips. But would all this be enough?

My hesitation was based on the fact that all these things are subject to change. The income stream from both the 401K and Thrift Saving were dependent upon the stock market, and we all know how volatile that can be! You'd think Social Security and the federal pension would be safe, but are they? Congress has made multiple attempts to change both. They greatly reduced the value of the federal pension plan in the 1980s by moving part of it to a stock-based plan, and have made continuous attempts to do the same with Social Security. They call these programs and Medicare "entitlement programs" and point out that all are underfunded and in danger.

The truth is that working people pay for these programs through hefty payroll deductions. I will not live long enough to collect all the money I paid into Social Security and you probably won't either. In my opinion, the reason the programs are in trouble is because Congress violated their fiduciary responsibility. Instead of investing the money taxpayers put into the programs, Congress spent the money on other things. How they handle these funds would be against the law if Congress were a private company.

I set all my fears aside when I remembered: The future is guaranteed to no one. My husband and I both retired in July, 2010. I was pleasantly surprised to find out that it really was enough; it all worked out. I'm very grateful that IRS and Social Security put money in my bank account every month and I no longer have to work. At age

67, I finally achieved my original goal to be a housewife, if not a mother.

When I look back at the ups and downs of my quest for financial freedom, it seems a miracle that I ever made it. How did I get from being a bag lady at age 48 to where I am now? In retrospect, it's easy to see where I made some choices that certainly took me off the path to financial freedom, but somehow I always managed to find my way back. My mother's explanation was: "Cream rises." My own analysis is somewhat different.

Reading the paragraphs in this memoir, my work life sounds somewhat chaotic. In reality it was actually very trendy. In the '60s I was a social worker, in the '70s a bureaucrat, in the '80s an entrepreneur, and in the '90s a technocrat. Except for the "survival" jobs, most of the work I did was in addition to my day job and can be grouped into two categories: things I did for fun or jobs to make money so I could do or get something I wanted. My real motivation was never the money; it was the financial freedom to do what I wanted to do, buy what I wanted to buy, and to have fun. I'd been rich and I'd been poor, but most of my life I'd had upper income jobs, supplemented by all the part-time work I did. What I had going for me was my willingness to work for what I wanted. I never had trouble making money, only trouble hanging on to it.

At age 45, my life could best be described by the chorus of Janice Joplin's song, "Me & Bobbie McGee," By that time I had no money, no home, no job, no savings, no insurance and no retirement. It seems to me that Maslow's hierarchy of needs, a theory in psychology proposed by Abraham Maslow in his 1943 paper "A Theory of Human Motivation," explains the choices I made between age 45 and 67.

First, the IRS seasonal job met my physiological needs, the physical requirements for human survival. With these needs met, my focus turned to safety. Aside from the salary, the primary reason I accepted the federal job offer was because of the benefit package: job security, paid annual and sick leave, insurance, retirement pension, Social Security and savings (401K.). The need for love and belonging led to my marriage. The actions I took to position myself for retirement led to the self-confidence to retire, and retirement has led to self-actualization. But understanding what motivated me explains why I did what I did, but not how I did it. I know that persistence and luck played a role but for the actual method I'd have to look a little further.

If you have never read *The Richest Man in Babylon*, I highly recommend that you do so. Written by George Samuel Clason, this book dispenses financial advice through a collection of parables set in ancient Babylon. Published in 1926, the advice is as relevant today as it was when then. When I read *The Richest Man in Babylon*, I realized I had found the answer to how I went from bag lady with a mink coat to affluent retired housewife. I stumbled on to the method, but I wish I'd read the book a long time ago. Following is my summary of the advice Clason gives:

1. Pay yourself first. Save at least 10% of what you earn. I did this when I put money into my 401K plan.
2. Learn to "get by" on only a percentage of what you earn. This happened automatically when I started saving money for retirement.
3. Let your money work for you by taking advantage of compounding interest. In the book Clason calls interest income "golden children" and advices us not to eat our golden children.
4. Carry insurance against disaster in all its forms. That's why I have health and dental insurance, property and flood insurance, and life and long-term care insurance.
5. Make your home a profitable investment. I did this by buying and remodeling a house we could afford and by not withdrawing all the equity.
6. Make certain that your investing activities will provide you with an income in your old age. If you can, work for the government or a company that provided a pension, Social Security and a 401K.
7. Increase your ability to earn. I went back to school and took advantage of training offered.

8. Have a good advisor. I hired a financial planner and followed the advice.

As I said earlier, the accumulation of money was never my goal. The goal was what the money could buy. Therefore, my life-long pattern was to accumulate money until I had enough to get what I wanted: a house, a car, a vacation, etc. I was consistently putting money into savings and taking it out of savings. For example, the eight years I was married to my first husband, I put $100 a month into savings each and every month. When I left, there was $500 in the account. This habit insured that I had money to meet emergencies or to buy something, but did nothing to insure wealth over the long term because I consistently ate my golden children.

I changed at age 48 when my goal became enough money to retire. I quit eating my golden children. I paid off debt and put money into a tax-deferred retirement account where the money could work for me. Can you imagine how wealthy I would be today if I started saving at age five?

I am now happily retired and spend my time traveling, quilting and creating fiber art. I've given away a number of quilts but never tried to sell any because, at this time, I have everything I need to make me happy.

CPSIA information can be obtained
at www.ICGtesting.com
Printed in the USA
FFOW04n1946010516
23698FF